CW00349455

BIOGRAPHY OF BRITISH TRAIN TRAVEL

A JOURNEY BEHIND STEAM & MODERN TRACTION

DON BENN

First published in Great Britain in 2017 by
Pen & Sword Transport

An imprint of Pen & Sword Books Ltd
47 Church Street, Barnsley, South Yorkshire S70 2AS

ISBN 978 1 47385 844 2

Pen & Sword Books Ltd incorporates the imprints of Pen & Sword Archaeology, Atlas, Aviation, Battleground, Discovery, Family History, History, Maritime, Military, Naval, Politics, Railways, Select, Social History, Transport, True Crime, and Claymore Press, Frontline Books, Leo Cooper, Praetorian Press, Remember When, Seaforth Publishing and Wharncliffe.

For a complete list of Pen & Sword titles please contact
Pen & Sword Books Limited
47 Church Street, Barnsley, South Yorkshire S70 2AS England
E-mail: enquiries@pen-and-sword.co.uk
Website: www.pen-and-sword.co.uk

Design and typesetting
by Juliet Arthur, www.stimula.co.uk

Printed and bound in India by Replika Press Pvt. Ltd.

CONTENTS

PREFACE

The idea for this book came to me when I realised how many unfinished or unpublished articles were sitting on my PC. It surely wouldn't take me long to put them all together and add a few more illustrations and train running logs would it? Well that was back at Christmas 2014 when I was doing my annual project list for the coming year and I didn't actually finish everything until the end of September 2015. Some chapters didn't really fit into what was supposed to be a trawl through my long years of recording the railway scene and so they were rewritten or abandoned. The end result is I feel quite well balanced; I could have added more, but didn't do so in order to keep the book to a reasonable size and also to keep back material for a more in depth look in later books. This applies particularly to Southern steam and to my travels in Europe. The bias in this book is towards my two main railway passions of train running performance and all matters Southern. I hope that the reader will be able to find something of interest to delve into when a quiet moment presents itself.

INTRODUCTION

I often hear the phrase 'railways are in my blood' and it would be nice to think that this applies to me too as railways have dominated my life, but it does not. However engineering IS in my blood. My father spent his life in the motor trade and could and did build a car engine from a block, plus he tuned rally cars for a team which won various events in the 1950s and 60s. His father built the first successful automatic steering gear mechanism for yachts whilst working for a company in Bromley, Kent. It goes back even further as the family bible tells me that the Benn tribe worked in the Woollen Mills in Halifax in the 1830s, moving south at the turn of the nineteenth century. Railways were there somewhere though, as one uncle built and ran live steam 'O' gauge engines and another worked with steam on the railways in the 1950s. Running nights at the home of the 'O' gauge uncle became a regular feature in my youth once we had moved to Bromley in 1950 and inevitably I dawdled on the footbridge at Bromley South on the way to and from those enjoyable evenings so long ago. And that really was where it all started in the days before Kent Coast Phase One electrification when Sammy Gingell was producing his incredible efforts with steam engines from the huge variety still around then. Arrival on the footbridge to join the gang invariably coincided with an 'Arthur' standing on the old platform 2 with a down train to the Kent Coast. If you add to this the family outings to Dover to visit two ageing aunts on my mother's side of the family (which included some French blood, no doubt explaining my love of France) which also always saw us spending time in the docks and on the beach where we could watch the diminutive B4 class 0-4-0 tanks working their way slowly along the front between the Western and Eastern Docks, or the 'C' and 'O1' Class 0-6-0s shunting the docks, then I suppose you could say that railways were also in my blood. During those visits we would often stay in a caravan at Hawthorn Farm, Martin Mill from where my brothers and I would sometimes catch the train down into Dover for unofficial visits to the shed and docks area. It was when returning to Dover Priory station after one of these outings that we encountered Bulleid Pacific No.34091 *Weymouth* in original condition waiting to work a train to London. The friendly engine driver invited us up onto the footplate and the memory of that hot cab with the hum of the dynamo and the fireman opening and closing the steam-operated fire hole doors will stay with me always. He asked where we were going and I

My earliest surviving photo. 34085 on the down Golden Arrow at Bromley South in about March 1960.

C Class 0-6-0 No 31720 shunting Dover Docks in July 1960.

34100 *Appledore* on the up Golden Arrow passing Polhill Box in August 1960.

34089 *602 Squadron* before being rebuilt on the turntable at Dover shed in July 1960.

am sure that if it had been Canterbury and not Martin Mill then we would have stayed on the footplate for the ride. Chapter Twenty-Two gives a flavour of what it is like to actually ride on the footplate of a steam engine on the main line.

Then there were the family picnics by Austin Seven or Morris Ten, always accompanied by my father's pride and joy, the primus stove, in a biscuit tin to protect it from the wind. This device was developed in the desert; my father served with 'Monty' in the Eighth Army and took part in the battle at El Alamein, one of the turning points of the Second World War. This brewing contraption produced passable cups of tea to go with our sandwiches and cake. Most frequently these outings were to the piece of land next to Blackbrook Bridge at Bickley Junction where my father would cadge water from the signalman on the box up on the Chislehurst line, or to the hills above the SE Main line at Polhill where the day usually ended by seeing the up *Golden Arrow* Pullman.

And so the early days of this young railway enthusiast progressed and developed with the purchase of my first Ian Allan combined volume in 1958 with the realisation that steam existed outside our little world of Dover and Bromley. Visits to London by train from Bromley North and South had already started before it dawned on me that steam had a limited life. Sunday 14 June 1959 was a very sad day for the Bromley South gang as this was the last day of steam to the Kent Coast. I still have full record of the proceedings that evening as No 34001 *Exeter* worked the last down Ramsgate and L1 Class 4-4-0 No 31753 the last down Dover. Only the boat trains and a few others would remain at Bromley South and soon my horizons would broaden into steam in Europe and elsewhere, into wider railway interests including so called 'modern traction', and things narrow gauge, the latter holding a particular fascination for me. This book attempts to cover at least some of my long obsession with railways.

Don Benn
Southampton
September 2016

Chapter One

Kent Rover – 11 September 1960

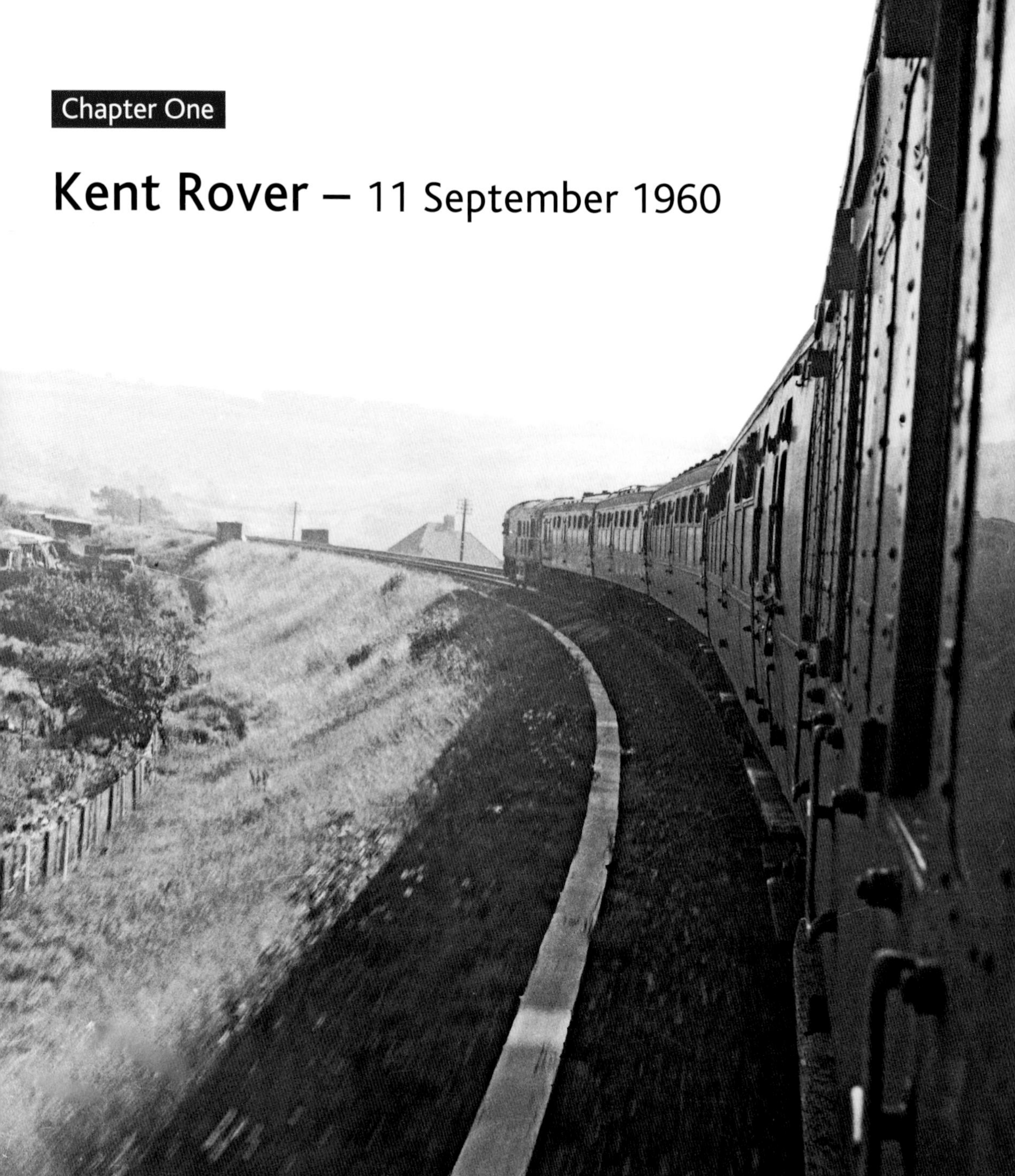

Sulzer class 24 D5000 climbs past Buckland with the 9.10 am Charing Cross to Ramsgate.

"We had covered no less than 329 miles by rail and all for the 10 shillings and sixpence cost of a Kent Rover ticket"

202

Table 27—continued **LONDON, SHEERNESS-ON-SEA, MARGATE, RAMSGATE, DOVER PRIORY, DEAL and SANDWICH** — Table 27

Sundays—continued

Down		am	am		am	am	am	am	am		am	am	am	am	am	am
Notes						9 52 am Herne Hill; Calls Beckenham Jn. 10 1, St. Mary Cray 10 18 am	To Dover Priory arr 12 5 pm		10 39 am from Sheerness-on-Sea				Ω Calls New Cross 9 51, St. Johns 9 54, Lewisham 9 56, Blackheath 9 58, Kidbrooke 10 1, Eltham (Well Hall) 10 4, Eltham Park 10 6, Falconwood 10 8, Welling 10 11, Bexleyheath 10 14, Barnehurst 10 17, Stone Crossing Halt 10 27, Greenhithe 10 29, Swanscombe Halt 10 32, Northfleet 10 35, and Higham 10 47 am.			
66 London Victoria	dep		9 40		9 49						1010			1015	1028	
62 London Charing Cross	dep							9 40					9 39			
62 " Waterloo	"							9 43					9 41			
62 " Cannon Street	"															
62 London Bridge	"							9 48					9 46			
62 Woolwich Arsenal	dep							10 3								
62 Dartford	"							1015					1023			
62 Gravesend Central	"							1025					1039			
Strood	"							1040					1057			
Bromley South	dep		9 57			10 9					1027			1032	1047	
Swanley	"											1038		1041		
Farningham Rd. & Sutton-at-Hone														1046		
Longfield for Fawkham and Hartley														1051		
Meopham														1055		
Sole Street														1058		
Rochester								1044					11 1	11 7		
Chatham			1024			1043		1047			1054	1059	11 5	1111		
Gillingham	arr		1027			1047		1050			1057	11 2	11 8	1114		
Gillingham	dep		1029	1032		1047		1051			1058	11 3	11 9	1115		
Rainham								1055						1120		
Newington								11 0						1127		
Sittingbourne	arr			1043				11 5			11 9	1115	1119			
Sittingbourne	dep			1050							1110					
Kemsley Halt				1054							1114			1134		
Swale Halt				1058							1118			1138		
Queenborough				11 3							1123			1143		
Sheerness-on-Sea	arr			1110							1128			1147		
Sheerness-on-Sea	dep	1018					1039									1118
Queenborough		1023					1043									1123
Swale Halt		1028					1048									1128
Kemsley Halt		1031					1051									1131
Sittingbourne	arr	1036					1059									1136
Sittingbourne	dep			1043			11 0	11 5			1111	1116	1120			
Teynham							11 5	1110								
Faversham	arr			1053		11 5	1111	1116					1129			
Faversham	dep			11 1		11 6		1117	1118				1130			
Whitstable & Tankerton			1054		11 4	1116		1127			1130	1136	1141		1146	
Chestfield & Swalecliffe Halt			1058					1130			1134	1139	1144			
Herne Bay			11 3		1111	1123		1136			1139	1145	1150		1155	
Birchington-on-Sea			1113			1134		1145			1150	1155	12 1			
Westgate-on-Sea			1116			1139		1150			1155	1159	12 4			
Margate	arr		1120		1125	1142		1153			1158	12 2	12 8		1211	
Broadstairs			1127		1131	1150		12 0			12 5	1210			1218	
Dumpton Park			1131		1135	1154		12 3			12 9	1214				
Ramsgate			1134		1138	1157		12 6			1212	1217			1223	
Selling	dep								1123							
Canterbury East				1116					1133							
Bekesbourne									1139							
Adisham				1124					1144							
Aylesham Halt				1127					1147							
Snowdown & Nonington Halt									1150							
Shepherd's Well				1132					1154							
Kearsney				1138					12 0							
Dover Priory	arr			1142					12 5							
Martin Mill	arr			1210												
Walmer	"			1215												
Deal	"			1220												
Sandwich	"			1229												

Down		am		am	am	am	am		am	pm	am	am	am	am	pm
Notes		Victoria to Ramsgate	Buffet Car	Dep Blackfriars 10 45 am, calls Elephant and Castle 10 48 am, Peckham Rye 10 55 am, Nunhead 10 57 am, Catford 11 1 am, Bellingham 11 3 am	10 52 am Herne Hill; Calls Beckenham Jn. 11 0 am St. Mary Cray 11 15 am	To Dover Priory arr 1 4 pm	Dep New Cross 10 44 am, calls Lewisham 10 48 am, Blackheath 10 56 am Charlton 11 1 am, Plumstead 11 8 am, Abbeywood 11 11 am			11 39 am from Sheerness-on-Sea		Ω Calls New Cross 10 51, St. Johns 10 54, Lewisham 10 56, Blackheath 10 58, Kidbrooke 11 1, Eltham (Well Hall) 11 4, Eltham Park 11 6, Falconwood 11 8, Welling 11 11, Bexleyheath 11 14, Barnehurst 11 17, Stone Crossing Halt 11 28, Greenhithe 11 30, Swanscombe Halt 11 33, Northfleet 11 36, and Higham 11 47 am.			
66 London Victoria	dep	1040									1110		1115	1130	
62 London Charing Cross	dep								1040			1039			
62 " Waterloo	"								1043			1041			
62 " Cannon Street	"														
62 London Bridge	"								1048			1046			
62 Woolwich Arsenal	dep						11 6		11 3						
62 Dartford	"						1120		1115			1124			
62 Gravesend Central	"								1125			1140			
Strood	"								1137			1153			
Bromley South	dep	1057		11 9	11 6						1127		1132	1147	
Swanley	"												1141		
Farningham Rd. & Sutton-at-Hone													1146		
Longfield for Fawkham and Hartley													1151		
Meopham													1155		
Sole Street													1158		
Rochester									1141			1156	12 7		
Chatham		1124							1144		1154	12 0	1211	1216	
Gillingham	arr	1127			1141				1147		1157	12 3	1214		
Gillingham	dep	1129	1132		1142				1148		1159	12 4	1215		
Rainham									1152				1220		
Newington									12 0				1227		
Sittingbourne	arr		1143	1147					12 5			1215		1228	
Sittingbourne	dep		1150						12 7						
Kemsley Halt			1154						1211				1234		
Swale Halt			1158						1215				1238		
Queenborough			12 3						1220				1243		
Sheerness-on-Sea	arr		1210						1225				1247		
Sheerness-on-Sea	dep					1139									1216
Queenborough						1143									1221
Swale Halt						1148									1226
Kemsley Halt						1151									1229
Sittingbourne	arr					1156									1234
Sittingbourne	dep		1143	1148		1157			12 5			1216		1229	
Teynham						12 2			1210						
Faversham	arr		1153		12 0	12 8			1216		1219	1225		1238	
Faversham	dep		1153		12 0				1216	1218	1221	1226		1239	
Whitstable & Tankerton		1154		12 5	1210		1219		1226		1231	1236		1249	
Chestfield & Swalecliffe Halt		1158							1229		1235	1239			
Herne Bay		12 3		1212	1217		1226		1235		1240	1245		1256	
Birchington-on-Sea		1213			1227				1245		1250	1256		1 7	
Westgate-on-Sea		1216			1231				1249		1255	1259		1 10	
Margate	arr	1220		1225	1235		1238		1252		1258	1 3		1 14	
Broadstairs		1227		1232	1242		1246		1259		1 6			1 21	
Dumpton Park		1231		1236	1246		1250		1 2		1 10			1 24	
Ramsgate		1234		1239	1249		1253		1 5		1 13			1 28	
Selling	dep									1223					
Canterbury East			12 8							1233					
Bekesbourne										1239					
Adisham			1216							1241					
Aylesham Halt			1219							1247					
Snowdown & Nonington Halt										1250					
Shepherd's Well			1224							1254					
Kearsney			1230							1 0					
Dover Priory	arr		1234							1 4					
Martin Mill	arr									1 32					
Walmer	"									1 38					
Deal	"									1 43					
Sandwich	"									1 52					

2 Second class only

Sundays

1961 Summer timetable.

Completion of Phase 1 of the Kent Coast electrification programme in June 1959 meant the end of steam from Victoria to Ramsgate and Dover via the Medway towns. It was greeted with some dismay by the small band of youthful enthusiasts who used to frequent the footbridge which crossed the country end of Bromley South station, and from which we used to watch the seemingly endless procession of Maunsell 4-4-0s, King Arthurs and Moguls mixed up with BR standard class 5s and of course the Bulleid Pacifics, which worked mainly on boat trains between London and Dover or Folkestone. These were to last another two years, but in the immediate aftermath of June 1959 they didn't have the same appeal as our beloved Ramsgates at three minutes before each hour worked by such gems as *Sir Meleaus de Lile or Sir Dinadan*. However every cloud has a silver lining and the completion of this phase of electrification saw the introduction of a short lived Kent Rover ticket giving unlimited travel over the newly electrified lines from London and Bromley South to Ramsgate, Dover and Sheerness. The temptation to spend the day bashing up and down the lines in the newly built CEP and BEP stock was irresistible. The pattern of these trips was broadly similar each time: Bromley South to either Ramsgate or Dover, then a diesel or steam hauled train between the two and a return to Bromley South, followed by the same in reverse with a side trip to

4 CEP 7115 at Dover Priory on the 8.40 am from Victoria (8.57 am from Bromley South).

Sheerness for good measure. The standard hour train service, especially on Sundays, was quite generous, as follows:

xx40 each hour	semi-fast Victoria to Ramsgate and Dover Priory, dividing at Gillingham
xx40 each hour	Charing Cross to Ramsgate stopping service
xx15 each hour	Victoria to Sheerness stopping service
xx39 each hour	stopping service Sheerness to Dover Priory

A similar pattern operated in the up direction.

On Sunday mornings extra trains operated to cater for Londoners wishing to visit the Kent coast resorts for the day, with a similarly enhanced evening return service. This seems incredible to us now but was in the days before universal ownership of the car and when the train was used for such outings. In fact some extra trains remained in the South Eastern timetable into the early 1980s. The timetable extract shows the Sunday morning down service from the summer 1961 timetable.

So on a warm and sunny Sunday, 11 September 1960, a happy band of three brothers set off to walk to Bromley South and catch the 8.57 am to Dover Priory. These trips were in the days before serious train timing could be undertaken but records of times to the nearest half minute were kept and survive today. These included some estimates of speeds which must be taken very much with a pinch of salt as they were arrived at by the basic method of counting the time taken to cover twenty-three rail joints and converting this to miles per hour! In those days of course welded track was still in the future. Our train was comprised of twelve coaches: 4CEP+4BEP+4CEP, with the front eight coaches including the buffet unit running through to Ramsgate. As we were going to Dover we travelled in the rear unit, 7115, one of the main batch built in 1959.

We left Bromley South 5 minutes late and ran non-stop to Chatham in 24 minutes, regaining a minute and a half on the fairly tight 25½ minute schedule for the 23.4 miles, with some lively running down past Farningham Road. After Chatham the train called at Gillingham, where it divided with the front eight coaches soon away to run fast to Whitstable. Our portion with 4CEP 7115 departed, still 3 minutes late to call at Sittingbourne, Faversham and all stations to Dover Priory except Selling, Bekesbourne and Snowdown, these stations being served by the following 9.39 am from Sheerness. Further lively running saw us into Dover Priory two minutes early, where we crossed the footbridge to Platform 2 in time to see the 10.38 am to Victoria depart also with another 4CEP. Our unit 7115 would sit at Dover until the 1208 pm up and we were to see it again later at Gillingham when joining up with our 1210 pm from Ramsgate. However, I digress and much to our delight the 9.40 am stopping service from Ashford which had arrived at 1026 was hauled by BR Standard class 4 2-6-4 tank and was still

BR Standard class 4 2-6-4 tank 80066 at Dover Priory on the 9.40 am local from Ashford.

BR Standard class 4 2-6-4 tank 80066 takes water at Dover Priory after working the 9.40 am local from Ashford.

standing in Platform 3. Soon afterwards the engine uncoupled to take water at the far end of the platform. We hadn't expected to see much steam that day so this was a bonus.

Dover had very special memories for us, as it was a favourite destination for family summer outings and holidays in the 1950s, nearly always undertaken by car, mostly in an ancient Austin Seven into which were crammed the complete family of Dad, Mum and four children. I can still remember the drama which accompanied the climb of Dover Hill out of Folkestone, with my father adjusting the fuel mixture from controls on the dashboard to ensure that we made it to the top! Later a Morris 10 was acquired to make the journey slightly more comfortable. However the best and most enduring memory of Dover was when, on returning from an illicit shed bash one hot summer day, we encountered unrebuilt WC class 4-6-2 34091 *Weymouth* simmering away in Platform 3 with a train for Victoria via Faversham. We were invited onto the footplate by the kindly, elderly driver. I can still feel the warmth of the enclosed cab and hear the hum of the turbo generator while we watched the fireman using the pedal to open and close the steam-operated firebox doors. All too soon the driver was preparing to depart but not before asking us where we were going. Alas we were bound for our campsite at Martin Mill but I am quite sure that if we had been going to Faversham we would have got a cab ride in that superb engine. That would have been around 1957 so unfortunately before the days when a camera was carried.

Back to 1960 and our next train was the 9.10 am Charing Cross to Ramsgate, which during the week was still steam hauled

Sulzer Class 24 D5000 at Ramsgate after arrival with the 9.10 am from Charing Cross.

by a Bulleid light Pacific and would be until June 1961, but on Sundays was diesel hauled. It rolled in on time at 10.55 am behind BR Sulzer class 24 Bo-Bo D5000. It had run fast from Waterloo to Folkestone Central in 87 minutes, a very undemanding schedule for the 69.2 miles, and then called all stations to Margate (1203 pm) via Ramsgate, reached at 11.47 am.

I can't recall whether any coaches were dropped at Dover but we climbed slowly up the steep climb past Buckland to Guston tunnel with eight fairly lightly loaded coaches of Bulleid- and Maunsell-built stock including a Bulleid 4-set at the front of the train. The gradients on this climb vary but are as steep as 1 in 68 in places. Steam runs up here were always exciting and the inside of the train was often filled with smoke if the youthful travellers returning to base at Martin Mill kept the windows open! The BR Sulzer class 24s were not really intended for the Southern as initial deliveries were for operation in the Crewe and Derby areas, but fifteen of the first twenty were diverted for use on the Southern to help out until the completion of the Kent Coast electrification, Phase 2. The heavy weight (75 tons) of these locos was too much for the Chief Civil Engineer to accept and they had to have their boilers removed, later to be restored so they could provide train heating when working in tandem with the indigenous Class 33s which were only fitted for electric train heating.

On arrival at Ramsgate an early lunch was taken, no doubt from the contents of our duffle bags, which included such delights as spam sandwiches and tizer! We then continued on to complete the first circular trip back to Bromley South on the 1210 pm from Ramsgate with 4CEP 7153 and 4BEP 7007, both from the original main production batch for Phase 1 of the Kent Coast electrification in 1959. These units were powered by English Electric 250hp EE 507 traction motors, two mounted on each nose end axle of the motor coach at each end of the unit, producing a nominal 1,000 hp per 4-coach set, or 3,000 hp per 12-car train. 7153 was prototype for the refurbishment of the CEPs to modern standards in 1975. The original CEPS and BEPS, with express gearing, had a balancing speed on level track of about 72mph and a maximum speed of 90mph, though this could often be exceeded with keen drivers trying to make up time. They could be very rough riding. This was alleviated to some extent by the fitting of hydraulic dampers quite early on, and later by replacement of the original MK 1 bogies with MK 2 then MK 4. They did, however continue to provide an entertaining ride right up until final withdrawal in 2005 – real trains indeed!

2 HAP 5629 at Sittingbourne with the 3.16 pm from Sheerness.

Anyway, back on the 1210 Ramsgate, we left on time and called all stations to Whitstable, then fast to Gillingham, where we arrived two minutes early, despite being checked outside behind the front portion from Dover, which as stated earlier was 7115 again. We had come up from Whitstable, 23.2 miles, in 26 minutes, with some very fast running, up to around 90mph past Teynham, where I can still recall the train crashing violently around over the crossings at the station. The continuation to Bromley

4 EPB 5235 in the car sheds at Ramsgate.

South was more sedate, arriving on time at 149 pm. A quick turnaround saw us on the 157 pm back to Sittingbourne, with another CEP/BEP/CEP formation, numbers unrecorded. We left 4 minutes late and were on time at Chatham, after another very fast run of just 21 minutes for the 23.4 miles, and speed in excess of an estimated 90mph at Farningham Road. In the early days especially, drivers seemed to enjoy getting the best out of their new trains, or maybe some were just trying to prove that the electrics could do anything that Sam Gingell could do with a Standard '5' or Bulleid light Pacific? We got off at Sittingbourne to have a side trip to Sheerness on the 250 pm train with 2HAP 5629, returning at 316 pm with the same unit and then continuing to Ramsgate on the 404 pm train, which had started as the 240 pm from Charing Cross and was comprised of an 8-coach train of 2-car 2HAP units. We left Sittingbourne 3 minutes late and arrived at Ramsgate 2 minutes early at 503 pm. Here we continued our clockwise circuit on to Dover on a fine late summer evening by catching the 547 pm to Charing Cross, eight coaches hauled by Class 33 Bo-Bo D6516.

These engines would give many years of mostly reliable service all across Southern territory and some would last into preservation. Rated at 1550 hp with four Crompton Parkinson traction motors they were very useful all round machines. This train would continue, calling at

Class 33 D6516 at Ramsgate with the 5.30 pm to Charing Cross.

Folkestone Central, Shorncliffe, Sandling and then fast to Waterloo in a very easy timing of 87 minutes for the 64.7 miles. It seems incredible today that so many trains omitted to call at Ashford, but it was then just a small market town, as indeed it still was when we lived there for a few years from 1968 in the early years of marriage.

So onto the final leg of our day out, by catching the 7.10 pm Dover Priory to Victoria as far as Gillingham. By now the Sunday evening return from a day out at the coast was well underway so our train had the full 12-car CEP/BEP/CEP formation of units 7143, 7011 and 7123. We left a minute late and arrived at Gillingham on time where we had decided to change into the following 7.10 pm Ramsgate to Victoria train which at this peak time on a Sunday evening was running separately from the Dover train. We were however surprised when it ran in 2 minutes late at 8.17 pm, not with the expected 12 CEP/BEP formation but with units, 6075, 6069, 5615, 6071 and 5314, a 12-coach train of 2HAPs and one 4EPB, the latter without toilet facilities. Despite the suburban gearing of 5314 we only took twenty-six minutes from Chatham to Bromley South arriving on time at 8.50 pm at the end of an interesting and varied day out in beautiful late summer sunshine. We had covered no less than 329 miles by rail and all for the ten shillings and sixpence cost of a Kent Rover ticket. So it was a happy gang of brothers who walked the last mile home from Bromley South to enjoy a belated and no doubt very burnt Sunday lunch.

Chapter Two

Tonbridge – 20 May 1961

H class tank No 31308 brings an empty stock train possibly from Bricklayers Arms on the through road.

"The variety of engine classes at Tonbridge as late as 1961 is remarkable"

U1 class 31893 leaves Tonbridge on an afternoon train for Redhill.

This was one of a number of visits to Tonbridge using a half day excursion ticket from Bromley South, on this occasion just three weeks before the end of steam on the South Eastern main line. Even after that event, Tonbridge would still see quite a lot of steam hauled trains, as those to Oxted, Brighton and Redhill would last a few more years, with the latter being the last to succumb to dieselisation in January 1965. Tonbridge team (73J) shed also closed in 1965.

The pictures tell the tale of a long afternoon and early evening photographing the various comings and goings. My record-keeping then wasn't very good, but I have pieced together the captions from my brief notes and a copy of the winter 1960/196 Southern timetable. Train headcodes and knowledge of which engines tended to work on the various lines have enabled me to produce an almost complete story of the trains we saw. At that time most main line trains from Charing Cross to Ashford and Dover and Ramsgate at 10 minutes past alternate hours were hauled by class 33 diesels and the 20 minutes past each hour trains from Charing Cross to Hastings had been operated by the new diesel electric multiple units since 1957. Continental Boat Trains to and from Victoria and Folkestone or Dover were still almost entirely worked by Bulleid light Pacifics and would be until 11 June 1961. These always caused a wave of excitement amongst the many 'spotters' on the platform that afternoon, as can be

Schools class No 30936 *Cranleigh* arrives at Tonbridge with a train from Redhill.

34089 602 Squadron brings the 2.20 pm Folkestone Harbour to Victoria through Tonbridge past 80153.

Schools class 30928 *Stowe* backs to Jubilee sidings to collect the stock for an afternoon train to Brighton.

Schools class 30936 *Cranleigh* awaits departure from Tonbridge with an unknown working.

seen in the shot of 34089 on the 2.20 pm from Folkestone Harbour. Redhill trains arrived generally at around ten minutes to each hour returning at various times, but roughly hourly intervals.

'H' class 0-4-4 tanks had charge of the shuttles to and from Oxted which were infrequent so we can be fairly sure that 31544 was working the 4.38 pm to Oxted and 31005 had arrived at 4.55 pm on the 4.04 pm from Oxted. Trains from Brighton arrived at 27 minutes past each hour returning at ten past. These were hauled by BR class '4' 2-6-4 tanks or Maunsell Moguls, as were the Redhill trains. There were also infrequent trains to Maidstone West, some of which worked through from Redhill.

The identity of the trains in two of the pictures is uncertain. First the shot of 'H' class No 31308 according to the headcode discs should show a train from Bricklayers Arms and it is certainly an empty stock working as it is running on the down through road. Possibly more likely though it has come from Jubilee sidings just to the west of the station and may be bound for Paddock Wood to work to Maidstone West or Hawkhurst. Secondly the shot of Schools class No 30936 *Cranleigh* appears to show it on a train to Redhill as it appeared from there earlier as shown in another shot. However the headcode discs indicate something else and I suspect that this train may be the 2.41 pm through train from Margate to London Bridge which No 30936 had just taken over, possibly from a class 33 diesel loco. This train ran via Redhill and eventually got to its destination at 6.47pm.

The variety of engine classes still at Tonbridge as late as 1961 is remarkable. The Schools class had all gone by the end of 1962, but the Wainwright 'H's, dating from 1904 lasted incredibly another two years.

H class 31544 on the stock of an Oxted train entering Tonbridge.

H Class No 31005 shunts the empty stock of a push-pull train from Oxted.

34004 *Yeovil* passes slowly through Tonbridge with the 3.30 pm Victoria to Folkestone Harbour boat train.

BR class 4 tank 80064 in an afternoon train to Maidstone West.

34077 *603 Squadron* brings the 2.25 pm Dover Marine to Victoria boat train through Tonbridge with 31893 on the left.

Schools class 30928 *Stowe* brings the empty stock of an afternoon train to Brighton into Tonbridge.

28 October 1961.
31518 departs from Dunton Green with the Flyer for the last time.

"These much enjoyed trips instilled in me and one of my brothers a lifelong interest in trains"

14 October 1961. 31530 at Dunton Green.

Many Sunday afternoon excursions into Kent from our home in South East London in the 1950s taken by Austin seven or Morris ten for family picnics often seemed to take us to or through Westerham. Here the statue of General Wolfe on the Green was pointed out with a potted history of this distinguished soldier and his early demise in the course of the victory over the French at Quebec always recounted by my father, to the extent that it has never been forgotten. Many lazy hot afternoons were spent looking down from Westerham heights watching the red two-car push-pull set with its little tank loco pottering up and down the line and disappearing tantalisingly as it approached Westerham station. Some 120 years after Wolfe's death the good people of Westerham, having got tired of waiting for the South Eastern Railway to act, promoted their own bill in Parliament to build a railway from Dunton Green to Oxted via Westerham. The South Eastern Railway became involved but opposed the extension from Westerham to Oxted where it would have joined with the LBSCR's line. So the line opened on 6 July 1881, quite late in the railway era. Westerham station was a gem, much photographed during my many visits in the last year of operation. It had been little changed over the years, retaining many of the original buildings until the end, which came on 28 October 1961.

The final timetable in 1961 was slightly curious, as on Mondays to Fridays it was essentially a commuter railway with no trains during the middle part of the day. The Saturday timetable included the morning commuter trains but then ceased

Table 65—*continued*

LONDON, BROMLEY NORTH, ORPINGTON, DUNTON GREEN, WESTERHAM, SEVENOAKS, TONBRIDGE and TUNBRIDGE WELLS

Down	am	am	pm						Saturdays—*continued*										pm			
LONDON		②	②			②	②	②	②	②	②		②	②					②	②	②	②
„ **Charing Cross** .. dep	1150	1157	..	..	1220	..	1219	1228	..	1242	1250	..	1 0	..	1 10	1 20	..	..	1 28	1 37	1 57	..
„ **Waterloo**	1153	1159			1223		1221	1230		1245	1252		1 2		1 13	1 23			1 30	1 39	1 59	
„ **Cannon Street**	..	..	12 5	1215	..	1218	..	..	..	..	..	1 2	..	1 13	..	..	..	..	..	..	..	2 12
London Bridge	12 0	12 4	12 8			1221	1226	1234		1250	1256		1 6	1 16					1 34	1 43	2 4	2 17
New Cross	..	1210	1214	..	..	1227	1233	1240	..	1256	1 2	..	1 12	1 23	..	..	..	..	1 40	1 49	2 10	2 23
St. John's		1212						1242											1 42		2 12	
Hither Green	..	1215	1219	..	..	..	1238	1245	..	1 1	1 7	..	1 17	1 27	..	..	..	..	1 45	1 54	2 15	2 27
Grove Park		1219	1222				1241	1249		1 5	1 10		1 20	1 31					1 49	1 57	2 19	2 31
Sundridge Park			1225				1244			1 8				1 34						2 1		2 34
Bromley North .. arr	..	..	1228	..	..	..	1247	..	..	1 10	..	..	..	1 36	..	..	..	..	..	2 3	..	2 36
Elmstead Woods		1222	Stop			1236	Stop	1252			1 14		1 23	Stop					1 52		2 22	Stop
Chislehurst	..	1224	..	..	..	1239	..	1256	..	..	1 16	..	1 26	..	..	..	..	..	1 54	..	2 24	..
Petts Wood		1228				1242		1 0			1 20		1 31						1 58		2 28	
Orpington arr	..	1231	..	..	..	1246	..	1 3	..	..	1 24	..	1 34	..	..	..	..	..	2 1	..	2 31	..
Orpington dep		1234				1246		1 4					1 34						2 4		2 34	
Chelsfield	..	1237	②	..	..	1250	..	1 7	..	..	..	..	1 37	②	..	..	..	..	2 7	..	2 37	②
Knockholt		1240	pm			1253		1 10					1 40	pm					2 10		2 40	pm
Dunton Green	..	1246	1250	..	..	1 0	..	1 16	1 20	..	..	..	1 46	1 50	..	..	..	..	2 16	..	2 46	2 50
Chevening Halt .. dep			1252						1 22					1 52								2 52
Brasted Halt	..	..	1257	..	..	..	..	..	1 27	..	..	..	..	1 57	..	..	..	..	..	..	..	2 57
Westerham .. arr			1 1						1 31					2 1								3 1
Sevenoaks arr	..	1250	..	1243	1253	1 4	pm	1 20	..	..	..	..	1 50	..	..	1 53	..	..	2 20	..	2 50	..
Sevenoaks dep				1243	1253	—	1 17									1 53		2 0				
Hildenborough	..	..	..	..	1 0	Stop	..	..	..	..	..	..	..	..	..	..	..	2 8	..	..	..	..
Tonbridge arr	1239			1253	1 5	pm	1 26					1 39			1 52	2 3		2 15				
Tonbridge dep	..	..	..	1253	1 6	1 10	..	..	..	..	..	1 39	..	..	..	2 4	2 10	..	..	..	..	..
High Brooms						1 19											2 19					
Tunbridge Wells Central arr	..	..	..	1 3	1 16	1 25	..	..	..	..	..	1 50	..	..	..	2 14	2 25	..	..	..	..	..
Tunbridge Wells West .. „						1 30											2 30					

Down	pm								Saturdays—*continued*										pm			
LONDON		②	②			②	②				②	②	②	②	②				②	②	②	②
„ **Charing Cross** .. dep	2 20	2 28	2 37	..	3 10	2 57	3 8	3 20	..	..	3 28	3 37	3 57	..	4 8	4 20	..	4 32	4 28	4 37	4 57	5 8
„ **Waterloo**	2 23	2 30	2 39		3 13	2 59	3 11	3 23			3 30	3 39	3 59		4 11	4 23		4 35	4 30	4 39	4 59	5 11
„ **Cannon Street**	..	..	..	..	..	..	..	..	..	..	..	..	..	..	..	..	..	..	..	..	..	..
London Bridge		2 34	2 44			3 7	3 17				3 34	3 44	4 4		4 17			4 41	4 34	4 44	5 4	5 17
New Cross	..	2 40	2 51	..	..	3 13	3 23	..	..	..	3 40	3 51	4 10	..	4 23	..	..	..	4 40	4 51	5 10	5 23
St. John's		2 42									3 42		4 12						4 42		5 12	
Hither Green	..	2 45	2 55	..	..	3 18	3 27	..	..	..	3 45	3 55	4 15	..	4 27	..	..	..	4 45	4 55	5 15	5 27
Grove Park		2 49	2 59			3 21	3 31				3 49	3 59	4 19		4 31				4 49	4 59	5 19	5 31
Sundridge Park			3 2				3 34					4 2			4 34					5 2		5 34
Bromley North .. arr	..	..	3 4	..	..	..	3 36	..	..	..	..	4 4	..	..	4 36	..	..	..	..	5 4	..	5 36
Elmstead Woods		2 52	Stop			3 24	Stop				3 52	Stop	4 22						4 52	Stop	5 22	Stop
Chislehurst	..	2 54	..	..	..	3 27	..	..	..	..	3 54	..	4 24	..	..	..	..	..	4 54	..	5 24	..
Petts Wood		2 58				3 31					3 58		4 31						4 59		5 28	
Orpington arr	..	3 1	..	..	..	3 34	..	..	..	..	4 1	..	4 34	..	..	..	..	..	5 2	..	5 31	..
Orpington dep		3 4				3 34					4 4		4 34						5 4		5 34	
Chelsfield	..	3 7	..	..	..	3 37	②	..	..	..	4 7	..	4 37	..	..	..	..	..	5 7	..	5 37	②
Knockholt		3 10				3 40	pm				4 10		4 40						5 10		5 40	pm
Dunton Green	..	3 16	..	..	..	3 46	3 50	..	..	..	4 16	..	4 46	4 50	..	..	..	..	5 16	..	5 46	5 50
Chevening Halt .. dep							3 52							4 52								5 52
Brasted Halt	..	..	..	..	..	..	3 57	..	..	..	..	..	..	4 57	..	..	..	..	..	..	..	5 57
Westerham .. arr							4 1							5 1								6 1
Sevenoaks arr	2 53	3 20	..	..	3 44	3 50	..	3 52	..	..	4 20	..	4 50	..	..	4 53	..	5 11	5 20	pm	5 50	..
Sevenoaks dep	2 53				3 44			3 52								4 53		5 11	—	5 33		
Hildenborough	..	..	..	..	..	..	..	3 59	..	..	..	..	..	..	..	..	..	5 20	Stop	..	..	..
Tonbridge arr	3 3		pm		3 55			4 4				pm				5 3		5 26	pm	5 43		
Tonbridge dep	3 4	..	3 10	..	..	..	..	4 4	4 10	..	..	4 38	..	..	..	5 4	5 10	..	5 38	..	..	..
High Brooms			3 19						4 19			4 46					5 19		5 46			
Tunbridge Wells Central arr	3 14	..	3 25	..	..	..	..	4 14	4 25	..	..	4 50	..	..	..	5 14	5 25	..	5 50	..	..	..
Tunbridge Wells West .. „			3 30						4 30			4 55					5 30		5 55			

② Second class only

Goods shed and station at Westerham, August 1961.

until late morning, then running an hourly service through to the last train at 7.50 pm from Dunton Green. The lunch period involved an extra train to connect with the 12.18 pm from Cannon Street and 12.28 pm from Charing Cross as in those days the City worked on Saturday mornings, as indeed I did when in my first job in Croydon. So for me it was often the case of cycling to work complete with a sandwich lunch, tizer bottle and camera and then on to Westerham for the afternoon. Saturday afternoons also saw a change of engine after the 4.23 pm from Westerham so two of the regular engines could normally be seen. Sundays was the only day when trains ran all day hourly right through to the 9.50 pm from Dunton Green.

These much enjoyed trips instilled in me and one of my bothers a lifelong interest in trains, Southern in general and at that time Westerham in particular so we found our own way there frequently, often by train all the way, but sometimes by means of a red RT bus on London Transport Route 146 from Bromley North to Downe and then a long walk via Biggin Hill and down the hill to Westerham. Why was the Downe route London Transport but the Godstone Route 410 London Country Buses with green low height RLHs? Perhaps because it was ex East Surrey Traction Company Route S10 from Reigate to Bromley via Westerham, designed to give a connection from Oxted, originally the intended terminus of the line from Dunton Green. Biggin Hill airfield ceased to be operational in 1958 when the Gloster Meteors of 41 Squadron moved to Coltishall, but officers and pilots continued to be trained there until 1995, when it finally became non-military; it still exists as a significant international private airfield. I don't suppose many aircrew follow the footsteps of their wartime predecessors and drink in the little pub in Jail Lane though.

Arrival at Westerham normally meant sandwiches and tizer, but if taken on the train would involve close scrutiny by

OPPOSITE: Saturday afternoon train service.

31530

22 October 1961. 31263 bowls along near Brasted with a train from Dunton Green.

the conductor who was very proud of his ancient red ex Railmotor set. Crumbs on the floor were not allowed! So, many happy days were spent photographing and travelling on this line until we learned the awful truth that the Transport Minister Earnest Marples had ignored the recommendations of the TUCC and approved closure, despite there being over two hundred regular daily users. No doubt the preferred line of the South London Orbital, now the M25, played a large part in this decision, plus of course his financial interests in the road building industry. It now covers a lot of the track bed of this railway, from before Chevening until well after Brasted.

Very little remains of this charming little line. However at Dunton Green Station the elaborate subway shelter covering the footpath under the curved branch and tracks still exists and is in use.

OPPOSITE:
14 October 1961. 31530 near Chevening with an afternoon train from Dunton Green to Westerham.

At Brasted the stationmaster's house and old coal yard are still there, right next to the M25. The coal yard now appears to be a scrap yard but is usually locked and may not be in use. It was here in 1918 that my father-in-law started his fifty-year railway career as station lad, one of the four staff. Right up to his recent death at

Brasted Station c1922. Station master with SE&CR hat and to his left my father in law, referred to in the text, looking as though he may have just been picking apples!

Brasted Halt on 22 October 1961.

the age of 98 he still had vivid recollections of life on this line and elsewhere on the South Eastern and Chatham and later the Southern in Kent. After the stationmaster noticed his apples going missing, he was given the task, with the booking clerk, of guarding the trees. Of course they knew where the apples were going! The trackbed of the line can also just be made out crossing the Westerham eastern bypass, but Westerham Station itself has disappeared under light industrial development.

The last few weekends before closure were spent trying to photograph every aspect of the branch, although Saturdays were hampered by the need to work at my father's garage in West Wickham in the morning, serving petrol and washing cars in order to earn enough money to pay for the train and bus fares to get to the line and to buy the film for my woefully inadequate camera. Our first photos of the branch were taken in August 1960 with an old Kodak 6x9 folding camera which produced quite presentable results as long as we remembered the limitations of a maximum shutter speed of 1/60th of a second! This was replaced in September 1961 by a basic 35mm camera of East German origin and it was this that was used to record the last few weekends before closure, trying to photograph every aspect of the branch. On Saturday, 14 October, in bright conditions, 'H' class 31530 working Tonbridge duty 301 together with push-pull set 610 presided in the morning, with 31324 (Tonbridge duty 310) in the afternoon.

22 October 1961. 31263 near Brasted with a Dunton Green to Westerham train.

22 October 1961. 31263 entering Brasted Halt.

31530 entering Westerham, 14 October 1961.

WESTERHAM STATION

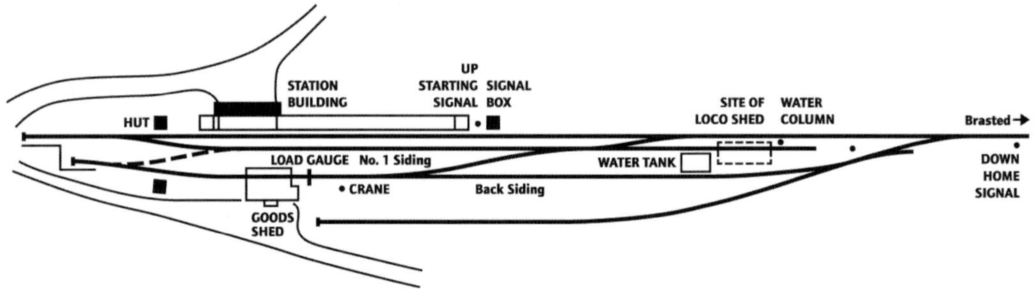

August 1961.
31177 entering Westerham.

October 1961.
31530 arriving at Westerham.

31177 at Westerham. August 1961.

31263 at Westerham on 22 October 1961, one week before line closure.

28 October 1961. 31739 arrives at Dunton Green in the Westerham platform.

The following Sunday, 22 October, the morning engine was 31518 on Tonbridge duty 302 followed by a very clean 31263 (duty 303) in the afternoon, again with push-pull set 610. Sunday was the only day with a full service, so the changeover at Dunton Green was at 12.40 pm, rather than at 4.40 pm on Saturdays. Presumably 31263 was already earmarked for preservation, and had perhaps been specially prepared. Despite a cold and damp day, there were many enthusiasts in evidence. Something that many of us wondered about was what the white concrete cable covers were doing lying by the lineside next to the branch line at and near Dunton Green. Perhaps the Southern Region Board had wrongly anticipated the Minister's decision on the future of the line and were planning electrification, partly off the back of the recently completed Kent Coast scheme, stage 2.

And so to Saturday, 28 October 1961, the last day. It dawned a beautiful autumn day, dry bright and sunny, and remained so all day. I treated myself to a colour negative film for the occasion and recorded the scene until the light went in the evening, when black and white was used in a vain attempt, without flash, to record the last rites. At Elmers End 2EPB 5706 was waiting on the 1.11 pm to Sanderstead. This train would travel over track now used partly by the Croydon tramlink. We then boarded a 4EPB on the 1.10 pm Elmers End to New Cross, where Hastings Unit 1037 was photoed on the 1.20 pm ex Charing Cross, followed immediately by E5000 on a van train on the up main and

28 October 1961. H tank 31518 passes over the reins to D1 31739.

D6539 with a 6-car ECS, set 277, on the up slow. We didn't know it at the time but this latter was to be the stock for the final trains to Westerham. No doubt someone will know where it originated, possibly Grove Park, or even Tonbridge. Another 4EPB took us on the 1.28 pm ex Charing Cross, arriving at Dunton Green at 2.16 pm. Soon 31518 with push-pull set 610, complete with last day 'Flyer' inscriptions, arrived on the 2.23 pm from Westerham.

There were murmurings of a Special on the down, so we quickly went to the London end of the up platform in time to photograph 'D1' class 4-4-0 No 31739 on the aforementioned 6-car set 277. This it proceeded to shunt to the up line and then onto the branch, where the whole train stood for a while in beautiful light next to 31518 having worked the last ordinary branch train, a scene that must have been recorded on yards of film. Certainly there was much rushing about by all and sundry to try to get the best shots before 31518 disappeared back to Tonbridge, and 31739 departed on the 2.50 pm to Westerham. The run round loop at Dunton Green could not cope with six cars, so during the afternoon, SR 'Q1' 0-6-0 No 33029 appeared and alternated with 31739 until the end of proceedings.

31739 faced Westerham and 33029 was facing out of the terminus, which produced some variety. For the record, 31739 worked the 2.50 pm, 4.50 pm and 6.50 pm from Dunton Green and 3.23 pm, 5.23 pm and 7.23 pm from Westerham, whereas 33029 operated the 3.50 pm,

28 October 1961. 31739 at Dunton Green.

5.50 pm and 7.50 pm from Dunton Green and the 4.23 pm and 5.23 pm from Westerham. Therefore the last train from Westerham was hauled by tender first 31739 and the last train of all on the branch, the 7.50 pm from Dunton Green, was hauled by 33029.

After an afternoon of walking the line and photoing, we had a round trip with 33029, and then finally travelled behind 31739 on the very last train from Westerham at 7.23 pm. Departure was an emotional moment with detonators and firecrackers exploding. On arrival at Dunton Green, we were invited onto the footplate to chat with the driver and fireman, and had our tickets signed by the driver, after which we said farewell and returned home by Southern Electric, as we had many times before.

The next day, Westerham gone but not forgotten, we were off to London by 4EPB and Circle Line, photoing a Maunsell 'N' and D6512 on engineers' trains at Spa Road, then A4 *Mallard* at the 'Cross', followed by a Sunday afternoon of Panniers, Halls, Castles and Kings at Paddington. What variety there was in the London area then. More film used on 'The Flyer' than anything else that year though!

The light fades at Westerham on the last day, 28 October 1961.

Chapter Four

Area 2 Rail Rover – Saturday, 28 April 1962

King Arthur class 4-6-0 30451 *Sir Lamorak* stands at Woking with the 8.46 am Salisbury to Waterloo semi-fast train.

"I have lost track of how many of these tickets I bought but a dozen survive in my ticket collection"

King Arthur class 4-6-0 30451 *Sir Lamorak* arrives at Woking with the 8.46 am Salisbury to Waterloo semi-fast train.

In the 1960s the Southern Region offered three local Area Rail Rovers each valid for a day within a defined area at a cost of ten shillings (50p today). To us hard up youngsters these tickets were too good to miss. The Area 2 Rover in particular was a big attraction as it covered the South Western main line from Waterloo to Woking as well as the Guildford to Redhill line, the latter being 100 per cent steam worked until the end of 1964. The line from Waterloo of course carried the steam hauled trains from Waterloo to Basingstoke, Salisbury and Southampton and beyond, many of which stopped at Woking and so were ideal for us ardent train bashers.

I have lost track of how many of these tickets I bought but a dozen survive in my ticket collection spanning the years from 1960 to 1964. Sometimes we would go out *en famille*, including my brothers and my father, and these trips tended to be track and unit bashes rather than chasing after steam as my father's interest tended more towards such things rather than the dying steam breed. However I realised in early 1962 that the days of the more interesting Southern steam classes were numbered and so I got together with a friend from my schooldays and we planned a day out which hopefully would give us runs behind at least one member of the King Arthur, Lord Nelson and Schools classes using information gleaned from our lineside sessions. No Internet or much else to help us in those days of course.

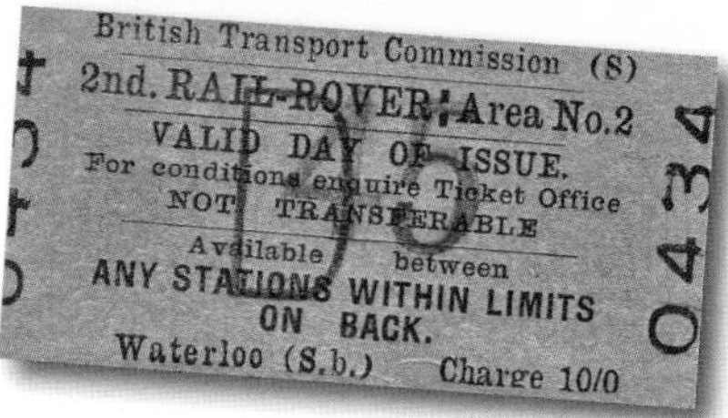

Area 2 Rail Rover ticket.

The day chosen was Saturday, 28 April 1962 and we met outside East Croydon station after I had arrived by RT bus on the dreaded Route 54. Our aim was to

73111 *King Uther* leaves Woking on the 09.54 Waterloo to Basingstoke while the driver of an S15 in the bay watches as his engine takes water.

30451 *Sir Lamorak* stands at Woking with the 8.46 am Salisbury to Waterloo semi-fast train.

kick off the day with steam which we duly did by catching the 9.11 am to London Bridge, a 3-coach train with super power in the form of unrebuilt Battle of Britain class 4-6-2 34057 *Biggin Hill.* This train had originated from Brighton at 7.17 am and ran easily on time with such a light load as to enable us to change to an EPB unit at London Bridge and arrive at Waterloo in good time for our first train on the South Western main line, the 9.54 am Basingstoke local which as expected was a BR class 5 4-6-0 on five coaches. It was a bright and sunny morning and 73111 coped without fuss with the standard 31 minute schedule for the Basingstoke locals as far as Woking. At Woking we had time to ponder our positioning to photograph our first up train of the day, and one of the highlights, as the train concerned, the 8.46 am from Salisbury to Waterloo (and 2.54 pm return), was a regular King Arthur turn, and what's more had been 30451 *Sir Lamorak* for many weeks prior to our day out. Indeed my first record of it appearing on that train in 1962 was 27 February and I had photographed it on the same turn many times in the intervening weeks. This means that it had probably worked the same Mondays to Saturdays duty for at least ten weeks though it had been displaced by late May and in the summer 1962 timetable the train had become a Bulleid unrebuilt light pacific duty.

We were not disappointed and *Sir Lamorak* duly ran into Woking a few minutes early in the up slow line, looking absolutely splendid in the morning sunshine and giving us plenty of time to take the master shot and get over the footbridge for a couple more photos before boarding the train for the run to

King Arthur class 4-6-0 30451 *Sir Lamorak* arrives at Waterloo with the 8.46 am Salisbury to Waterloo semi-fast train. The Pannier tank is waiting to remove the ECS of the up Royal Wessex and the Bulleid Pacific is on the 11.30 am to Bournemouth.

Waterloo. Off we went on time, crossing over to the fast line and accelerating well with a modest load of 225 tons. It proved to be the best run of the day and there was great excitement when my friend and I agreed that his stopwatch gave 11.8 seconds for the best quarter mile near Hersham; a very fine 76mph. As we were running early the engine was eased and then caught adverse signals from a train in front calling at Wimbledon. Even so the actual time up from Woking was just over 28 minutes or 26 minutes net for the 24.3 miles. As we ran into Waterloo four minutes early, a Pannier Tank was waiting to back into the stock of the up Royal Wessex and take it empty to Clapham Junction, and a rebuilt Bulleid light Pacific was waiting on the 11.30 to Bournemouth. Our elderly and friendly driver told us his name, Bert Cambray, from Salisbury shed, and he would be having a break before working back home on the 1 pm down, which we hadn't planned to catch.

Our next train was the 11.54 am Waterloo to Basingstoke; it turned out to be the same stock that *Sir Lamorak* had brought in. This time we were headed by an unrebuilt Bulleid light Pacific, our second of the day. It was 34091 *Weymouth* from Salisbury shed, which ran easily with this light train though putting in a little spurt after Byfleet Junction to equal the highest speed of the day, 76mph. The unrebuilt engines always seemed to me to be freer running than the rebuilds and sometimes would just run easily away with no change to the controls especially with light trains. So we gained over 3 minutes on the 31 minute schedule in a good time of 27 minutes 45 seconds. At Woking the driver was full of praise for his engine saying how good the Bulleids

WOKING TO WATERLOO

Date	28 April 1962					28 April 1962				28 April 1962			
Train	846 am Salisbury to Waterloo					1220 pm Eastleigh to Waterloo				515 pm Salisbury to Waterloo			
Loco	King Arthur Class 4-6-0 30451 *Sir Lamorak*					Lord Nelson Class 4-6-0 30862 *Lord Collingwood*				BR Standard Class 5 4-6-0 73117			
Load	5 coaches and 2 vans, 210 tons tare, 225 tons gross					5 coaches 165 tons tare, 175 tons gross				4 coaches and 2 vans 162 tons tare, 170 tons gross			
Weather	fine and sunny light SW wind					cloudy light SW wind				rain SW wind			
	miles	sched	mins	secs	speed	sched	mins	secs	speed	sched	mins	secs	speed
Woking	0.00	0.00	00	00		0.00	00	00		0.00	00	00	
West Byfleet	2.61		04	15	60		03	56	53		04	10	54
Byfleet Junction	3.89		05	28	66		05	17	60		05	27	61/64
Weybridge	5.14		06	34	69		06	35	58		06	42	62
Walton	7.21		08	21	73		08	35	64		08	35	67
Hersham	8.38		09	16	76		09	45	66/68		09	35	73
Esher	9.90		10	33	70		11	09	64		11	00	64
Hampton Court Jct.	10.95	14.00	11	30	68	13.00	12	11	63	14.00	12	02	60
Surbiton	12.25		12	44	62		13	28	62	16.00	14	15	
Berrylands	13.31		13	47	60		14	30	63		02	25	37
New Malden	14.51		15	00	62		15	40	64		03	53	57
Raynes Park	15.65		16	05	64		16	40	68		05	05	63
Wimbledon	17.10		17	43	sigs 47*		18	18	sigs 31*		06	25	64/67
Earlsfield	18.71		20	09	sigs 43*		20	46	50/53		08	00	65
Clapham Junction	20.36	25.00	22	05	53/43*	23.00	23	05	33*	11.00	09	41	sigs 43*
Queens Road	21.48		23	55	47		25	15	45		-	-	sigs 15*
Vauxhall	22.98		25	36	46		27	15	40/sigs 10*		15	28	sigs 31*
Waterloo	24.29	32.00	28	05		30.00	31	30		18.00	19	00	
					* brakes				* brakes				* brakes
	net time 26 minutes depart on time, arrive 4 early Driver Cambray, Salisbury Top Link					net time 27 minutes depart 7 late arrive 8 late				depart on time, arrive 1 late			

were if looked after, which of course this one would have been at that time as Salisbury shed had a reputation for good maintenance almost to the end of steam. When I worked at Waterloo in 1966 my job was to try to ensure that the steam sheds had enough running spares to keep their engines serviceable. It was always a pleasure to phone the stores clerk at Salisbury, one Fred Butcher by name if I remember correctly. He would answer the phone 'Salisbury Shed – hub of the Universe!' And he almost always had the spares I wanted for another shed. How different from Nine Elms who seemed to struggle all the time. The 159s now shedded at Salisbury diesel depot also have a reputation for being well looked after, so old traditions die hard.

Anyway back to 1962 and our Area 2 Rover. After alighting at Woking our next objective was the 1.24 pm from Waterloo which was booked a Schools class 4-4-0, but with no steam hauled train due back to London we opted for a ride on an up Portsmouth train with set of 4COR electric units which got us back in good time for the 1.24. This was five coaches headed by 30935 *Sevenoaks* which ran down to Woking nicely, just losing a few seconds on the schedule after being put onto the slow line at Hampton Court Junction for the 1.30 pm Waterloo to Bournemouth the pass. Acceleration from this check was good with

30862 *Lord Collingwood* stands at Woking on the 12.20 pm Eastleigh to Waterloo.

N15 class No 30451 *Sir Lamorak* leaves Woking with the 2.54 pm Waterloo to Basingstoke whilst a Merchant Navy rushes past on the 3 pm Waterloo to Exeter.

speed reaching 72 at West Byfleet. Our final objective of the day was to get hauled by a Lord Nelson class 4-6-0 and as luck would have it one was booked to head the 12.20 pm Eastleigh to Waterloo due away from Woking at 1.56 pm. Fortunately this was late otherwise we probably wouldn't have got across the footbridge at Woking in time after getting off the 1.24 pm down.

30451 *Sir Lamorak* leaving Woking with the 2.54 pm Waterloo to Basingstoke.

Our engine was 30862 *Lord Collingwood.* We left 7 minutes late for a good start and then steady run to London, somewhat spoilt by signal checks, though with a reasonable net time of just 27 minutes. At Waterloo the 2.54 pm local to Basingstoke awaited us hauled by the King Arthur which had given us such a good run up from Woking that morning. *Sir Lamorak* didn't need to exert himself to keep time to Woking, despite being turned onto the slow line at Esher to let the 3 pm West of England express go by, though this didn't actually pass the 2.54 until it was leaving Woking, the two trains making a fine sight in a flurry of smoke and steam.

As we had achieved all our objectives but didn't want to call it a day yet despite the deteriorating weather we decided on a trip to Redhill and back and so caught a train of 2Bill electric stock to Guildford to wait for the 4.33 pm to Redhill. Whilst waiting for our train at Guildford, LMS

WATERLOO TO WOKING

Date	28 April 1962					28 April 1962				28 April 1962			
Train	954 am Waterloo to Basingstoke					1154 am Waterloo to Salisbury				124 pm Waterloo to Salisbury			
Loco	BR Standard Class 5 4-6-0 73111					Unrebuilt WC Class 4-6-2 34091 'Weymouth'				Schools Class 4-4-0 30935 'Sevenoaks'			
Load	5 coaches 165 tons tare, 175 tons gross					5 coaches and 2 vans, 210 tons tare, 225 tons gross				5 coaches 165 tons tare 175 tons gross			
Weather	fine and sunny light SW wind					fine and sunny light SW wind				cloudy			
	miles	sched	mins	secs	speed	sched	mins	secs	speed	sched	mins	secs	speed
Waterloo	0.00	0.00	00	00		0.00	00	00		0.00	00	00	
Vauxhall	1.29		03	23	35		03	15	33		03	55	37
Queens Road	2.81		05	20	49		05	10	50		05	30	49
Clapham Junction	3.93	7.00	07	02	36*	7.00	06	46	41*	7.00	07	35	44*
Earlsfield	5.58		09	40	45		09	00	56		09	42	53
Wimbledon	7.24		11	42	50		10	41	59		12	00	sigs 36*
Raynes Park	8.64		13	20	60		12	13	57		13	53	45
New Malden	9.78		14	25	63		13	25	59		15	07	54
Berrylands	10.98		15	33	66		14	42	56		16	25	56
Surbiton	12.04		16	33	62		15	47	60		17	32	60/64
Hampton Court Jct	13.34	18.00	17	50	65	18.00	17	05	64	18.00	18	55	sigs 47*
Esher	14.39		18	50	63		18	10	65		20	08	sigs 20* to local line
Hersham	15.91		20	17	60		19	36	66		22	35	45
Walton	17.08		21	27	62		20	36	69/66		23	55	56
Weybridge	19.15		23	31	64		22	27	67		26	05	64
Byfleet	20.40		24	38	69		23	32	73/76		27	12	69
West Byfleet	21.68		25	46	66/sigs stop 0*		24	34	75		28	18	72
Woking	24.29	31.00	30	50		31.00	27	45		31.00	31	20	
	net time 29 minutes									net time 28 minutes			

Class 2 2-6-2 tank 41261 from Brighton shed arrived with a train from Horsham at 4.05 pm and a class 700 Drummond 0-6-0 No 30698 dating from 1897 was moving about the station and yard. We were very lucky indeed to see this as it was withdrawn a few days later. Soon after, our train drew in, four coaches behind Maunsell N class 2-6-0 No 31852 which took us without fuss to Redhill keeping time throughout, calling at all stations and running up to a sedate 53mph maximum speed down the bank to Dorking. We soon returned to Guildford on the 5.34 pm behind another Maunsell Mogul 31401 and then back to Woking where we were in time to see S15 class 4-6-0 No 30837 plodding slowly past with a heavy freight for the west. The Redhill to Guildford line was one of my favourites in the early 1960s and is covered in Chapter Seven.

And so to our final steam run of the day, a sprightly affair behind BR Standard class 5 4-6-0 No 73117 on the 5.15 pm Salisbury to Waterloo which ran to the Surbiton stop in 14 minutes 15 seconds with a nice maximum speed of 73mph. My notebook doesn't record how we returned home but suspect it was by a 2EPB unit to Elmers End and a walk from there. So ended an excellent day out with our cheap Rover ticket sampling a good variety of steam, including three classes which would all be gone by the year end.

Class 700 0-6-0 No 30698 at Guildford.

Chapter Five

1962 Summer Saturday on the Southern

21 July 1962. 34045 *Ottery St Mary* at Worting Junction with the 9.30 am Waterloo to Southampton Docks.

"I can only marvel at how well the operating departments and motive power depots kept up with demands on such a busy day"

After the end of steam on South Eastern main lines in June 1961, I turned my attention to other lines which still had some steam operation and it didn't take me long to work out that the place to be for a high level of action was on the South Western main line out of Waterloo. I soon discovered that the footpath by the main line at Wimbledon was within easy cycling distance and so this was where my long association with steam out of Waterloo started, in July 1961, though there had been the occasional foray before that using Area 2 Rail Rovers. I soon learned that motive power provision was dominated by Bulleid's pacifics and to a lesser extent by BR Standard classes Four and Five, but that a number of the more interesting classes still remained and would do for a while yet. By June 1962 I was going further afield and had gleaned enough information from the various railway magazines to realise that a summer Saturday by the lineside would allow me to see and photograph as many as a hundred or more steam hauled trains, including some regularly hauled by Maunsell's Schools, Nelsons and Moguls. So it came about that I spent every Saturday bar one in the 1962 summer timetable somewhere on the South Western main line, reached either by a long cycle ride or in a few cases by train. The exception was 28 July, where during the course of a Southern Region Rail Rover I was linesiding on the Somerset and Dorset.

The added attraction of Worting

21 July 1962 30934 *St Lawrence* passing Worting Junction with the 9.42 am Waterloo to Lymington Pier.

21 July 1962. 73110 *The Red Knight* passing Worting Junction with the 1.45 pm Exmouth, 2.35 pm Seaton to Waterloo.

21 July 1962 Worting Junction. 73047 on the 9.35 am Waterloo to Bournemouth passing 73089 on the 9.25 am Wimbledon to Weymouth.

The complete list of dates and locations is as follows:

9 June	Brookwood, Pirbright and Farnborough
16 June	Clapham Junction
23 June	Pirbright
30 June	Worting Junction
7 July	New Malden and Raynes Park
14 July	New Malden
21 July	Worting Junction and Wootton
28 July	Chilcompton
4 August	Pirbright and Farnborough
11 August	Clapham Junction, Wimbledon and Pirbright
18 August	Weybridge and Woking
25 August	Wimbledon, New Malden and Pirbright
1 September	Worting Junction and Wootton

Junction was the extra variety of through trains from places 'up north', though the local services between Waterloo and Basingstoke couldn't be seen here. This youthful enthusiast took full advantage of the good spots available nearby even to the extent of straying trackside – there was a much more laid back attitude to such things then. I was only ever challenged once but managed to talk my way out of that!

I have kept full records of all those amazing days and have chosen 18 August 1962 in the Weybridge and Woking areas as an example for this chapter, together with a few shots from 21 July at Worting. My camera was a 35mm East German Franka which produced some reasonable results depending on how the film developing was handled, though the colour shots taken on Gevaert film have needed a lot of work to make them just about acceptable.

The tables show what happened that warm summer day so long ago and I can only marvel at how well the operating departments and motive power depots kept up with demands on such a busy day. Some things can be highlighted such as the use of a BR class 4 2-6-0 No 76014 on one of the up Lymington Pier trains instead of the usual Schools class 4-4-0, and even

434 | **Table 35** | SATURDAYS

Table 35—*continued* **From LONDON to THE WEST OF ENGLAND—Saturdays—*continued***

		1	2	3	4	5	6	7	8	9	10	11	12	13	14	15	16
		am		am	am	am	am	am		am	am	am	am	am	am	pm	am
32 LONDON Waterloo	dep	8 3			8 35			8 54		9 0				10 15	1035		1045
32 Surbiton	"	8U22			8U54			9o12		9U18							
32 Woking	"	8U40			8 52			9U29		9 37			9 25				
Basingstoke	dep				9 40			10 0		10 9			1016				
Oakley													1025				
Overton													1031				
Whitchurch North													1037				
Hurstbourne													1042				
Andover Junction								10 25		10 34			1051				
Grateley													11 1				
Idmiston Halt													1110				
Porton													1112				
Salisbury	arr	9 47			10 28		1042	10 50		11 0			1122	11 46	12 5		1216
	dep	9 50			10 32		1045	10 54		11 4		1114		11 51	12 9		1219
Wilton South												1120					
Dinton												1130					
Tisbury												1138					
Semley												1147					
Gillingham												1154					
Templecombe				1057	11 10			11 32		11 42		12 5		12 28			
Milborne Port Halt				11 2								1211					
Sherborne				11 8				11 44				1217					
Yeovil Junction	arr			1116			1133			12 0		1225					
41 Yeovil Town	arr			1146			1146			12 13		1243					
	dep						1120			11 52	1152						
Yeovil Junction	dep						1135			12 2	1212						
Sutton Bingham Halt											1217						
Crewkerne											1226						
Chard Junction	arr										1239						
42 Chard Central	arr										1255						
	dep										1137						
Chard Junction	dep										1240						
Axminster	arr	11 2					12 4			12 32	1248						1 34
43 Lyme Regis	arr	12 0								1 4							2 16
	dep	10 10					11 8			12 10							1 14
Axminster	dep	11 3					12 6			12 34							1 39
Seaton Junction	arr	11 10								12 40							1 45
44 Seaton	arr	11 39								1 0							2 5
	dep	10 20						12 5		12 5							
Seaton Junction	dep	11 12						12U23		12 43							
Honiton		11 29						12 40								1 45	
Sidmouth Junction	arr	11 38					1231			1 5						1 52	
45 Sidmouth	arr	12 7					1 35			1 35						2 16	
45 Budleigh Salterton	"	12 22					1 47			1 47						2 34	
45 Exmouth	"	12 40					2 2			2 2						2 46	
45 Sidmouth	dep					11 7		12 20								1 14	
Sidmouth Junction	dep					12 8	1232	12U49		Stop						1 53	
Whimple						1216										1 59	
Broad Clyst						1223										2 6	
Pinhoe						1227										2 11	
St. James' Park Halt						1233											
Exeter Central	arr				12 20	1235	1248	1 5						1 38	1 55	2 19	
46 Exmouth	arr				1 13	1 13	1 41	1 41						2 12	2 41	3 16	
	dep				11 45		1215	1215	12 47					1 15	1 15		
Exeter Central	dep				12 24		1254	1 10	1 26					1 47	1 59		
Exeter St. David's					12 32		1 2	1 20	1 30					1 53	2 7		
Newton St. Cyres									1 40								
Crediton							1 15		1 47								
Notes		Until 25th August. Through Carriages to Exmouth, Sidmouth and Seaton			Until 1st September. Restaurant Car Waterloo to Exeter commences 14th July. Through Carriages to Ilfracombe and Torrington		Through Train from Portsmouth and Southsea, dep 9 3 am (Table 54)	Through Carriages to Ilfracombe and Plymouth	Restaurant Car Waterloo to Exeter	Through Carriages Waterloo to Sidmouth Exmouth and Seaton				Until 1st September. Through Carriages to Ilfracombe and Torrington	ATLANTIC COAST EXPRESS. Restaurant Car Waterloo to Exeter. Through Carriages to Padstow and Bude		Buffet Car Train Waterloo to Seaton. Through Carriages to Lyme Regis

		17	18	19	20	21	22	23	24	25	26	27	28	29	30	31
		am	am	pm	pm	pm	am	am	pm	pm	pm	pm	pm	pm	am	pm
32 LONDON Waterloo	dep	11 0	1115				1029	1145	12 5						1154	
32 Surbiton	"						1048								1148	
32 Woking	"						1125								1227	
Basingstoke	dep						1213								1 15	
Oakley							1224								1 24	
Overton							1229								1 29	
Whitchurch North							1236								1 36	
Hurstbourne							1241								1 41	
Andover Junction							1250								1 50	
Grateley															2 1	
Idmiston Halt															2 10	
Porton															2 12	
Salisbury	arr	1232	1242				1 15	1 22	1 35		1 49		1 58		2 22	
	dep	1235	1246			1256		1 25	1 40		1 52		2 1			
Wilton South																
Dinton						1 9										
Tisbury						1 17										
Semley						1 27										
Gillingham						1 35										
Templecombe						1 46		2 3			2 30		2 40			
Milborne Port Halt						1 53										
Sherborne						1 59							2 53			
Yeovil Junction	arr		1 33			2 7					2 46		3 2			
41 Yeovil Town	arr		1 44			2 14					3 14		3 14			
	dep		1 25		1 35						2 23		2 56			
Yeovil Junction	dep		1 34		1 44	Stop					2 48		3 3			
Sutton Bingham Halt																
Crewkerne					1 58											
Chard Junction	arr				2 12											
42 Chard Central	arr				2 39											
	dep				1 52											
Chard Junction	dep				2 13											
Axminster	arr				2 21								3 31			
43 Lyme Regis	arr															
	dep			1 14									3 5			
Axminster	dep			2 8	2 22								3 32			
Seaton Junction	arr			2 14	2 29											
44 Seaton	arr				3 30											
	dep			1 26								2 48				
Seaton Junction	dep			2 15								3 21				
Honiton				2 31								3 35				
Sidmouth Junction	arr			2 39				2 59				3 43				
45 Sidmouth	arr			3 26				3 26				4 15				
45 Budleigh Salterton	"			3 40				3 40				4 57				
45 Exmouth	"			3 58				3 58				5 11				
45 Sidmouth	dep	1 14														2 55
Sidmouth Junction	dep	2U10		2 40								3 44				3 55
Whimple				2 46												4 3
Broad Clyst				2 52												4 10
Pinhoe				2 57												4 15
St. James' Park Halt				3 4												
Exeter Central	arr	2 28	2 38	3 6					3 30		3 47	4 1	4 7			4 23
46 Exmouth	arr	3 16	3 16	3 35					4 26		4 26	5 11	5 11			5 11
	dep	1 45	2 15	Stop					2 49		2 49		3 36			Stop
Exeter Central	dep	2 34	2 46						3 36		3 53		4 10			
Exeter St. David's		2 41	2 52						3 44		4 0		4 19			
Newton St. Cyres											4 10					
Crediton											4 17					
Notes		ATLANTIC COAST EXPRESS. Restaurant Car Train Waterloo to Ilfracombe. Through Carriages to Torrington	Restaurant Car Waterloo to Exeter. Through Carriages to Plymouth, Padstow and Bude					Restaurant Car Train Waterloo to Exmouth. Through Carriages to Sidmouth	21st July to 1st September. Restaurant Car Waterloo to Exeter. Through Carriages to Ilfracombe and Torrington		Through Train Portsmouth and Southsea (dep 12 15 pm) to Ilfracombe and Torrington (Table 54)		Restaurant Car Train Brighton (dep 11 30 am) to Plymouth (Tables 28 and 54)			

Summer Saturday timetable.

18 August 1962. 34023 *Blackmore Vale* passing Woking with the 10.45 am to Seaton and Lyme Regis.

18 August 1962. 76014 near Woking with the 10.30 am Lymington Pier to Waterloo.

18 August 1962. 33040 at Hook Heath with the 3.14 pm Basingstoke to Woking.

18 August 1962. 30765 *Sir Gareth* running very fast approaching Woking with the 1.28 pm Lymington Pier to Waterloo.

SATURDAY 18 AUGUST 1962

Down Trains,Weybridge until 1025 am, Woking until 1215 pm and Hook Heath until 430 pm

Train	Engine	Load	Notes
720 am Waterloo to Weymouth	34017	9+1 van	
722 am Waterloo to Salisbury stopping train	not recorded		
730 am Waterloo to Padstow, Bude, Illfracombe and Torrington	34095	13	
803 am Surbiton to Okehampton car carrier	35018	11	
752 am Waterloo to Bournemouth West	73113	9	
800 am Waterloo to Southampton Docks	34031	9	Oceon Liner Express
803 am Waterloo to Sidmouth, Seaton and Exmouth	34073	12	
815 am Waterloo to Weymouth Quay	34059	13+1 van	Channel Islands Express
822 am Waterloo to Bournemouth Central	73083	11	
830 am Waterloo to Weymouth	34093	11	
835 am Waterloo to Ilfracombe and Torrington	73089	11	
845 am Waterloo to Lymington Pier	30902	10	
854 am Waterloo to Plymouth and Ilfracombe	34107	12	
900 am Waterloo to Sidmouth, Exmouth and Seaton	35019	12	
915 am Waterloo to Swanage	34094	10	
924 am Waterloo to Weymouth	73114	10	
935 am Waterloo to Bournemouth West	73084	10	
925 am Wimbledon to Weymouth	73119	10	
942 am Waterloo to Lymington Pier	30937	10	
954 am Waterloo to Basingstoke	31804	5+1 van	
1005 am Waterloo to Bournemouth Central	34087	-	
1015 am Waterloo to Illfracombe and Torrington	73110	-	
1030 am Waterloo to Weymouth	35012	13	
1035 am Waterloo to Padstow and Bude	73082	12	Atlantic Coast Express
1045 am Waterloo to Seaton and Lyme Regis	34023	11	
1054 am Waterloo to Swanage	34056	8	
1125 am Woking to Salisbury	30514	4	
1100 am Waterloo to Illfracombe and Torrington	35014	13	Atlantic Coast Express. Running very fast.
1105 am Waterloo to Bournemouth West	73087	9	
1115 am Waterloo to Plymouth, Padstow and Bude	34052	12	32 minutes late
1122 am Waterloo to Weymouth	30903	11	
1130 am Waterloo to Bournemouth West	D6549	10	10 minutes late
1145 am Waterloo to Exmouth and Sidmouth	35027	12	
1154 am Waterloo to Salisbury	30825	5+1 van	
1205 pm Waterloo to Illfracombe and Torrington	35002	11	
1214 pm Waterloo to Bournemouth West	34044	12	
1200 noon Waterloo to Lymington Pier	30921	10	25 minutes late
1230 pm Waterloo to Bournemouth West	35020	12	Bournemouth Belle Pullman Car Train
1235 pm Waterloo to Weymouth and Swanage	73112	12	
1242 pm Waterloo to Basingstoke	31635	5	
100 pm Waterloo to Plymouth, Illfracombe and Torrington	35006	13	
122 pm Waterloo to Bournemouth Central	35030	11	
124 pm Waterloo to Salisbury	31821	8	
130 pm Waterloo to Bournemouth West and Weymouth	34065	13	running very fast
222 pm Waterloo to Bournemouth West	34022	12	
230 pm Waterloo to Weymouth	34028	10	
254 pm Waterloo to Basingstoke	34048	5	
300 pm Waterloo to Plymouth, Illfracombe and Torrington	35009	12	
305 pm Waterloo to Exeter Central	34056	10	
320 pm Waterloo to Weymouth and Bournemouth West	34042	12	
325 pm Waterloo to Basingstoke	30834	12	Empty Stock
330 pm Waterloo to Bournemouth West	30861	11	
354 pm Waterloo to Basingstoke	30507	3	
354 pm Clapham Junction to Exeter Central	30839	7	Milk Train empty stock

SATURDAY 18 AUGUST 1962

Up Trains, Weybridge until 1025 am, then Woking until 1215 pm, then Hook Heath until 430 pm

Train	Engine	Load	Notes
637 am Basingstoke to Waterloo 808 am	73087	10	
604 am Southampton Terminus to Waterloo 822 am	34044	10	
722 am Eastleigh to Waterloo 858 am	D6549	11	
645 am Salisbury to Waterloo 921 am	34052	5+1 van	
555 am Weymouth Quay to Waterloo 933 am	73112	10+1 van	
812 am Basingstoke to Waterloo	30861	12	Empty Stock
824 am Basingstoke to Waterloo 0939	30823	8	
749 am Salisbury to Waterloo 944 am	35006	3	
720 am Bournemouth West to Waterloo 1000 am	35030	11	
630 am Exeter Central to Waterloo 1008	34056	12	travelling very fast
812 am Bournemouth West to Waterloo 1049 am	34022	11	
734 am Weymouth/715 am Swanage to Waterloo 1051 am	34065	12	Royal Wessex. Engine ex works
730 am Exeter Central to Waterloo 1108 am	35009	-	
846 am Salisbury to Waterloo 1116 am	34048	5	
920 am Bournemouth Central to Waterloo 1134 am	34047	12	
1035 am Basingstoke to Waterloo 1150 am	34042	12	
835 am Bournemouth West to Waterloo 1158 am	34028	12+1 van	
1008 am Southampton Docks to Waterloo 1206 pm	34006	12	Oceon Liner Express
903 am Templecombe to Waterloo 1219 pm	30839	5+1 van	
1000 am Bournemouth Central to Waterloo 1226 pm	35017	10	non stop
920 am Swanage to Waterloo 1239 pm	34021	10	non stop from Bournemouth
1008 am Bournmouth West to Waterloo 1244 pm	34105	12	did not call at Bournemouth Central
920 am Weymouth to Waterloo 1250 pm	35001	11	
1030 am Lymington Pier to Waterloo 1256 pm	76014	8	
930 am Exeter Central to Waterloo 105 pm	73115	12	through carriages from Sidmouth
1212 pm Basingstoke to Waterloo 126 pm	30507	5	
930 am Exmouth to Waterloo 138 pm	34058	10	
1206 pm Salisbury to Waterloo 151 pm	34005	7	
1040 am Bournemouth West to Waterloo 142 pm	34051	13	
1020 am Seaton to Waterloo 157 pm	34075	11	through carriages from Lyme Regis
809 am Torrington/810 am Ilfracombe to Waterloo 208 pm	35003	12	
1253 pm Basingstoke to Waterloo 204 pm	31804	5	
825 am Plymouth to Waterloo 215 pm	34035	10	
11 am Bournemouth West to Waterloo 211 pm	35011	10	
835 am Ilfracombe/910 am Torrington to Waterloo 237 pm	73085	10	
1143 am Lymington Pier to Waterloo 226 pm	30902	10	
1210 pm Bournemouth West to Waterloo 240 pm	73113	12	
11 am Weymouth to Waterloo 245 pm	34071	13	through carriages from Swanage
1125 am Weymouth to Waterloo 250 pm	35021	12	
810 am Wadebridge to Waterloo 310 pm	73082	13	through carriages from Mortehoe
830 am Padstow/930 am Bude to Waterloo 323 pm	35025	11	
1 pm Salisbury to Waterloo 339 pm	30824	3	
325 pm freight	33006	-	
128 pm Lymington Pier to Waterloo 345 pm	30765	10	travelling very fast
1030 am Ilfracombe to Waterloo 353 pm	34096	12	Atlantic Coast Express
338 pm freight	33005	-	
148 pm Bournemouth Central to Waterloo 404 pm	73088	11	non stop from New Milton
105 pm Bournemouth West to Waterloo 414 pm	34007	8	
1048 am Torrington to Waterloo 419 pm	34108	13	Atlantic Coast Express
314 pm Basingstoke to Woking 355 pm	33040	3	
123 pm Swanage to Waterloo 442 pm	34085	10	travelling very fast
220 pm Bournemouth West to Waterloo 444 pm	73084	11	travelling very fast

18 August 1962. 31821 on the 1.24 pm Waterloo to Salisbury.

more unusual King Arthur class 4-6-0 No 30765 *Sir Gareth* on the 1.28 pm from Lymington Pier substituted for Schools class No.30937 *Epsom* which had worked down on the 9.42 am train and running very fast past my spot at Hook Heath having made up all of the ten minute late start from Southampton.

The log of Schools class 30921 *Shrewsbury* shows that this too was struggling, maybe not surprising in this last year of such a famous class when they had no regular work except the summer Lymington Pier trains and one duty on Central division lines, involving the 5.25 pm from London Bridge to Reading via Redhill. The picture of 30934 *St Lawrence* at Worting Junction on 21 July is interesting as this engine had been substituted for 30936 *Cranleigh* by driver Bert Fordrey at Basingstoke and it then proceeded to reach 80mph down the hill to Winchester. 30902 *Wellington* though was a star performer that summer and appeared on every Saturday except 1 September, mainly on the 8.45 am down and 11.43 am up trains. What incredible reliability. The number of trains hauled by Standard Class 5s was notable and one in particular was unusual in that it was booked non-stop over the 98.55 miles from New Milton to Waterloo. This was the 1.48 pm from Bournemouth and was hauled variously by 73113 (23 June), LN

18 August 1962. 34047 *Callington* approaching Woking with the 9.20 am from Bournemouth.

18 August 1962. 30839 approaching Woking with the 9.03 am Templecombe to Waterloo.

18 August 1962. 73119 *Elaine* passing Weybridge with the 9.25 am Wimbledon to Weymouth.

18 August 1962. 35011 approaching Woking on the slow line at Hook Heath with the 11 am Bournemouth West to Waterloo.

18 August 1962. 30902 *Wellington* at Hook Heath with the 11.43 am Lymington Pier to Waterloo.

class 30857 (30 June), 73089 (14 July), 34007 (21 July), 73085 (4 August), LN class 30856 (11 August) and 73088 (18 August). The time of two hours one minute wasn't excessive but with most engines having a tender capacity of only 4,725 gallons I wonder if sometimes an extra stop was made at Basingstoke for water. The 10 am from Bournemouth was non-stop, though this was booked for Merchant Navy Pacific haulage and it was every day that I saw it except for 23 June when it was hauled by LN class No 30857 *Lord Howe.*

Timekeeping on these busy summer Saturdays generally wasn't too bad but sometimes up trains appeared in the wrong order, as the train log for 18 August shows. On that day the worst offender was the 12 noon down train to Lymington Pier which left Waterloo 19 minutes late after the engine didn't appear until 12.11 pm and so ran behind both the 12.05 and 12.15 down trains. It passed me running about 25 minutes late and only

Date	Saturday 18 August 1962
Train	12 noon Waterloo to Lymington Pier
Loco	Schools Class 4-4-0 No. 30921 *Shrewsbury*
Load	11 coaches, 365 tons tare, 385 tons gross
Timed by	Michael Hedges
Weather	Fine and sunny

	miles	sched	mins	secs	speed
Waterloo	0.00	0.00	00	00	
Vauxhall	1.30		05	35	sigs*/30
Clapham Junction	3.90	7.00	09	20	46/41
Wimbledon	7.20		13	53	
New Malden	9.75		17	03	
Surbiton	12.05		19	35	
Hampton Court Jct.	13.35	18.00	21	00	53
Walton	17.10		24	55	
Byfleet Junction	20.40		28	23	61
Woking	24.30	28.00	32	55	46
Brookwood	28.00		28	05	42
Milepost 31	31.00		42	32	40
Farnborough	33.25		45	58	tsr *20
Fleet	36.50		50	40	51
Winchfield	39.85		54	18	56
Hook	42.20		56	48	56/65
Basingstoke	47.80		62	20	61
Worting Junction	50.30	65.00	65	20	48
Wootton	52.50		68	05	43
Micheldever	58.10		74	25	64
Wallers Ash	61.70		77	39	69
Winchester City	66.50		82	05	63/68
Eastleigh	73.45		89	23	sigs *42/52
St Denys	77.15		96	23	sigs severe*
Southampton Central	79.25	98.00	101	55	
			net time 95¾ minutes		* speed restriction

18 August 1962. 34006 *Bude* approaching Woking with the 10.08 am Southampton Docks to Waterloo.

18 August 1962. 34096 *Trevone* approaching Woking with the up ACE, 10.30 am Ilfracombe to Waterloo.

18 August 1962. 30861 *Lord Anson* approaching Weybridge with the 8.12 am from Basingstoke to Waterloo.

18 August 1962. 35003 *Royal Mail'* approaching Woking at 81mph with the 8.09 am Torrington, 8.10 am Ilfracombe to Waterloo.

18 August 1962. 34028 *Eddystone* at Hook Heath with the 2.30 pm Waterloo to Weymouth.

18 August 1962. 35012 *United States Line* passing Woking with the 10.30 am Waterloo to Weymouth.

18 August 1962. 30937 *Epsom* heading the 09.42 am Waterloo to Lymington Pier past Weybridge.

18 August 1962. Immaculate 34065 *Hurricane* at Hook Heath with the 1.30 pm Waterloo to Bournemouth West and Weymouth.

18 August 1962. 30861 *Lord Anson* after passing Woking with the 3.30 pm Waterloo to Bournemouth West.

18 August 1962. 30834 near Woking with the 3.25 pm Waterloo to Basingstoke ECS.

18 August 1962. 35018 passing Weybridge with the 8.03 am Surbiton to Okehampton car carrier.

18 August 1962. 34059 passing Weybridge with the 8.15 am Waterloo to Weymouth Quay.

18 August 1962. 31804 on the 9.54 am Waterloo to Basingstoke passing Weybridge.

25 August 1962. 30902 *Wellington* passing Wimbledon with the 8.45 am Waterloo to Lymington Pier.

18 August 1962. 73088 *Joyous Gard* on the 1.48 pm Bournemouth Central to Waterloo, non-stop to Waterloo from New Milton.

18 August 1962. 30902 *Wellington* passing Weybridge with the 8.45 am Waterloo to Lymington Pier.

18 August 1962. Urie S15 No 30514 leaving Woking on the 11.25 am to Salisbury.

18 August 1962. 30903 *Charterhouse* passing Woking with the 11.22 am Waterloo to Weymouth.

18 August 1962. S15 No 30507 at Hook Heath with the 12.12 pm Basingstoke to Waterloo.

doing about 45mph as the train running log shows. At Southampton there was an argument between the driver and guard as the latter insisted on giving the driver a lost time ticket. Other trains did very well and my notes suggest that the immaculate 34065 *Hurricane* was running at about 70mph up the climb to milepost 31 on its 13-coach load working the 1.30 pm down, thus reflecting its apt name! It was fresh from a Light Intermediate overhaul on 28 July when it had done 234,559 miles, so that explains it.

The train running of 34023 *Blackmore Vale*, shown in one of the photographs working the 10.45 am down, was perhaps more typical as it took 96 minutes to Salisbury against the booked 91, but with many out of course checks and a top speed of 72mph. 35003 *Royal Mail* on the up train due at 2.08 pm did better, also taking 96 minutes but instead of the 105 minutes booked and again with many checks. It arrived just one minute late after a maximum speed of 81mph past me at Hook Heath, two miles west of Woking.

I hope that the lineside log and photos give a flavour of those captivating days over fifty years ago. My only regret was not travelling on one of the Lymington Pier trains behind Schools class 30902 *Wellington*.

21 July 1962. 30793 *Sir Ontzlake* entering Basingstoke with the 5.15 pm Salisbury to Waterloo.

Date	Saturday 21 July 1962
Train	515 pm Salisbury to Waterloo
Loco	N15 Class 4-6-0 No. 30793 *Sir Ontzlake*
Load	3 coaches 95 tons tare, 105 tons gross
Timed by	Don Benn
Weather	Fine and warm

	miles	sched	mins	secs	speed
Woking	0.00	0.00	00	00	
West Byfleet	2.61		04	07	50
Byfleet Junction	3.89		05	30	58
Weybridge	5.14		06	52	52
Walton	7.21		09	06	58
Hersham	8.38		10	17	64
Esher	9.90		11	46	60
Hampton Court Jct.	10.95	17.00	12	51	57
Surbiton	12.25	19.00	14	45	
	0.00	0.00	00	00	
Berrylands	1.06		02	15	40
New Malden	2.26		03	45	52
Raynes Park	3.40		05	00	58
Wimbledon	4.85		06	25	62
Earlsfield	6.46		08	15	52
Clapham Junction	8.11	11.00	10	21	*42/51
Vauxhall	10.74		13	53	40
Waterloo	12.14	18.00	17	00	

Chapter Six

South Western Suburban Railtour

30517 just after Raynes Park on the way to Chessington South.

"These were part of the clear out of many of the interesting classes which had survived on the Southern"

30585+30587 passing Wimbledon on the first leg of the tour, the 11 am Waterloo to Hampton Court.

This tour was run jointly by the Stephenson Locomotive Society and the Railway Correspondence and Travel Society to mark the withdrawal of the Beattie well tanks and the H16 class pacific tanks in December 1962. These were part of the clear out of many of the interesting classes which had survived on the Southern. The tour ran on Sunday, 2 December 1962 and was repeated two weeks later on 16 December. The engines were 1874 built class 0298 2-4-0 well tanks numbers 30585 and 30587, classified 0P and commonly known as the Beattie tanks after their designer. They had worked on the Wenford Bridge line in Cornwall until replaced by ex Great Western small pannier tanks numbers 1367, 1368 and 1369 in the autumn of 1962. Together with classmate 30586 all three were withdrawn from service after the tour on 16 December. Both 30585 and 30587 survived into preservation. The third engine involved, No.30517, was one of the five powerful pacific tanks classified 6F which dated from 1921 of Urie design for heavy freight and latterly used for shunting at Feltham, trip freight working and passenger empty stock duties in the London area. This engine was also withdrawn after the tours to join its four classmates which had gone at the end of November.

The tour, comprising 30585 double heading with 30587 on six coaches left Waterloo at 11 am and first operated to Hampton Court via East Putney and Wimbledon, where it was photographed by me and two of my brothers amongst many others on a very cold but bright morning. We then cycled to New Malden to get the

30587+30585 returning from Hampton Court past New Malden.

Wadebridge, 24 July 1962. 30587 with Ivatt 2MT tank 41272.

30517 approaching Raynes Park returning from Chessington South.

pair in lovely light returning on the second leg, the 12.50 pm from Hampton Court to Wimbledon Yard. We then moved to a position close to the Kingston bypass near Raynes Park to get a shot of 30517 working the next section, the 1.29 pm Wimbledon yard to Chessington South and the return working at 2.05 pm from Chessington, again to Wimbledon yard. Finally in fading light we moved to the field next to Carter's Seeds near Raynes Park to catch the pair of Beattie well tanks on the 2.44 pm from Wimbledon Yard to Shepperton before deciding to call it a day and cycle home to Shirley, near Croydon. For the record the final leg of this quite extraordinary tour was at 3.45 pm from Shepperton to Waterloo via Richmond. Not sure why we didn't travel on the repeat trip but it may well have been the usual problem at that time: a shortage of cash. Or maybe it was the latest friend of the other gender!

30585+30587 passing Carters Seeds at Raynes Park with the penultimate leg to Shepperton.

Chapter Seven

Redhill to Guildford

18 January 1964. 31800 leaves Betchworth past my favourite crossing with the 9.45 am Reading to Redhill.

"It was a good line for photography with barely a mile of level track and lovely scenery throughout"

20 April 1962. 30911 *Dover* leaves Reigate with the 11.35 am Redhill to Guildford.

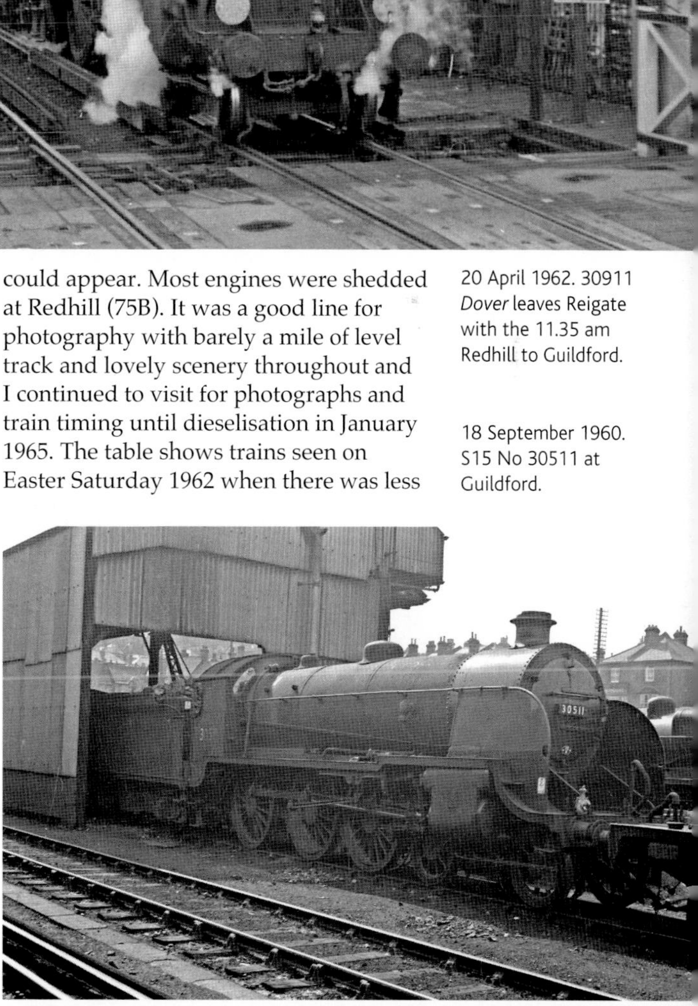

This line was one of my regular haunts in the 1960s as it was within cycling distance of home in Shirley near Croydon or could be accessed by bus and train via East Croydon. It had a reasonably regular train service still 100 per cent steam worked as late as 1963 though the Western Region would occasionally turn out a Hymek instead of the booked Manor on its one regular round trip from Reading.

There was also quite a lot of heavy freight and, in the summer, Inter Regional trains from Wolverhampton to Brighton and Hastings. These were normally 'Schools' hauled in 1962 but in 1963 were Great Western powered by Manors. The normal service trains and freight were almost all hauled by Maunsell 'N' and 'U' class 2-6-0s though the occasional BR class 4 tank or Standard class 4 2-6-0 could appear. Most engines were shedded at Redhill (75B). It was a good line for photography with barely a mile of level track and lovely scenery throughout and I continued to visit for photographs and train timing until dieselisation in January 1965. The table shows trains seen on Easter Saturday 1962 when there was less

18 September 1960. S15 No 30511 at Guildford.

LINESIDE LOG OF TRAINS IN THE BETCHWORTH/GOMSHALL AREA, EASTER SATURDAY 21 APRIL 1962

Time	Train	Engine	Number	Notes
1135 am	945 am Reading to Redhill	N class 2-6-0	31858	4 coaches and 2 vans
1145 am	Margate/Dover to Wolverhampton Low Level	N class 2-6-0	31868	12 coaches. Normally Schools class hauled
1150 am	Freight to Redhill	S15 class 4-6-0	30835	25 wagons
1155 am	Freight from Redhill	N class 2-6-0	31851	15 wagons
1235 pm	1105 am Reading to Redhill	N class 2-6-0	?	4 coaches
1250 pm	1234 pm Redhill to Guildford	U class 2-6-0	31615	4 coaches
1250 pm	Freight to Redhill	N class 2-6-0	31862	20 wagons
130 pm	1205 Reading to Redhill	U class 2-6-0	31790	4 coaches
145 pm	134 pm Redhill to Reading	N class 2-6-0	31858	4 coaches
210 pm	Freight from Redhill	N class 2-6-0	?	41 wagons
300 pm	1050 am Wolverhampton Low Level to Margate/Dover	Schools class 4-4-0	30930	13 coaches
325 pm	304 pm Redhill to Reading	U class 2-6-0	31790	4 coaches
330 pm	150 pm Reading to Redhill	N class 2-6-0	31861	3 coaches
425 pm	250 pm Reading to Redhill	N class 2-6-0	31868	4 coaches
430 pm	404 pm Redhill to Reading	N class 2-6-0	31859	4 coaches

freight than would normally be the case.

In those days of course linesides were kept clear of vegetation and there were many points where access could be obtained at foot crossings or bridges with nice views of the line. I had a lineside pass during the spring and summer of 1963 which helped though I never strayed far from my trusty Elswick Lincoln Imp bicycle. Although I have a fair selection of photos from 1962 and 1964, most of my lineside photography on this line was in the Spring and Summer of 1963 and was with medium format cameras capable of producing reasonable results; first a 6x9 Kodak folding camera and then from May 1963 an Agifold 6x6 camera, both obtained second-hand and both with limitations not helped by my sometimes dubious developing techniques.

From Redhill there was a bridge about a mile out on the 1 in 100 climb which proved a good vantage point especially for heavy freights slogging uphill from Redhill, and the view towards Reigate wasn't bad either, though neither shot was any good if the sun was out – not much of a problem in 1963 which was a pretty dismal year.

Reigate station was also good with some nice semaphore signals, but I didn't favour it much as most passenger trains stopped there and I preferred action shots. Further along was an overbridge near Dowde's Farm and then a crossing at Kemp's Farm which I liked as it had a nice background in both directions and then one of my favourite spots, the foot crossing on the Reigate side of Betchworth station. Here trains restarting from Betchworth would make nice actions shots especially in the morning if the sun was out. Moving along past Betchworth station, which was the top of the 1 in 116 climb from Deepdene, there were a few overbridges close to the A25 north of Brockham and then, between Deepdene

18 September 1960. N15 class 30457 *Sir Bedivere* at Guildford.

8 December 1963. 31622 backs to the shed at Redhill while 31797 waits to work the 2.05 pm to Reading.

8 December 1963. U class 31796 stands at Redhill on a frosty morning.

21 April 1962.
S15 class No 30835 near Betchworth with a heavy freight for Redhill.

21 April 1962.
The crew of 30835 work hard on a heavy freight to Redhill near Betchworth.

19 July 1962. Schools Class 30913 *Christs Hospital* arriving at Dorking Town with the 7.27 am Reading to Redhill.

19 July 1962. U class 31796 arrives at Dorking Town with the 8.35 am Redhill to Reading.

11 May 1963. N class 31868 struggles up the 1 in 100 out of Redhill with a heavy freight.

7 April 1963. N class 31852 approaching Betchworth with the 2.05 pm Redhill to Reading.

13 April 1963. N class 31820 has just topped Gomshall summit with a freight to Redhill.

13 April 1963. S15 30847 tops Gomshall bank with a van train from Redhill.

and Dorking Town, a useful footbridge. But it was Gomshall bank which held the greatest fascination for me with its 4 miles of 1 in 96/100 to a summit bridge at Hackhurst Farm, one of the few places where trains can still be photographed today with easy access and clear views, at least towards Guildford.

In the early 1960s there were many points where a determined young enthusiast and his bike could get to the line and full use was made of these Strangely I never ventured far beyond Gomshall, as if an iron curtain existed, and even station photographs are few in my collection. Perhaps Gomshall was the limit for my legs on the bicycle!

By the autumn of 1963 the appeal of trips for linesiding had faded somewhat and I undertook quite a long series of outings to ride and time the trains which lasted through to the end of steam, sometimes as a sideline from the L&SW main line but more often as an afternoon outing from home by an RT bus on Route 54 to East Croydon and then 2Hal or 2Bil electric stock from East Croydon to Redhill. Sundays were particularly favoured for these trips, maybe because then there was no television or girlfriend

13 April 1963.
N class 31864 on the 9.43 am Redhill to Guildford climbing Gomshall bank.

13 April 1963.
N class 31851 struggles past Betchworth at walking pace with a heavy freight for Redhill.

11 May 1963.
U class 31611 leaves Redhill with the lightly loaded 12.35 to Reading.

11 May 1963.
U class 31627 rolls down from Reigate with a heavy freight.

REDHILL TO GUILDFORD

Date	Sunday 24 November 1963					Sunday 15 December 1963			Sunday 22 December 1963		
Run Number	1					2			3		
Train	205 pm Redhill to Guildford					205 pm Redhill to Guildford			1236 pm Redhill to Guildford		
Loco	N class 2-6-0 No. 31817					BR Class 4 2-6-0 No. 76033			N class 2-6-0 No. 31866		
Load	3 coaches, 98 tons tare, 105 tons gross					4 coaches 136 tons tare, 140 tons gross			3 coaches 101 tons tare, 105 tons gross		
	miles	sched	mins	secs	speed	mins	secs	speed	mins	secs	speed
Redhill	0.00	0.00	00	00		00	00		00	00	
MP 23¾	1.25		03	11	30/37	04	00	24/36	03	10	31/28
Reigate	1.84	3.30	04	41		05	48		04	44	36
	0.00	0.00	00	00		00	00		00	00	
Betchworth	2.87	5.30	04	48	54/48	04	41	59	05	08	59/sigs 15*
	0.00	0.00	00	00		00	00		00	00	
Deepdene	2.60	4.30	04	16	53	04	27	54	04	32	54
	0.00	0.00	00	00		00	00		00	00	
Dorking Town	0.71		02	02	32/36	01	57	34/41	02	02	32/43
MP 34	4.18		08	20	34/52	07	42	39/51	07	26	41/58
Gomshall and Shere	5.43	10.30	10	37		09	47		09	11	
	0.00	0.00	00	00		00	00		00	00	
MP 36¼	0.99		02	15	35/55	02	45	32/56	02	31	35/53
Chilworth and Albury	3.94	7.30	06	26		06	43		06	38	sigs 20*
	0.00	0.00	00	00		00	00		00	00	
Shalford	1.83	4.30	03	33	46	03	40	44	03	26	52
	0.00	0.00	00	00		00	00		00	00	
Shalford Junction	0.72		02	08	27/38	02	00	35/39	01	47	41/28*/43
Guildford	1.91	6.00	04	39		04	26		04	12	

GUILDFORD TO REDHILL

Date	Sunday 24 November 1963					Sunday 15 December 1963			Sunday 22 December 1963		
Run Number	7					8			9		
Train	255 pm Guildford to Redhill					357 pm Guildford to Redhill			255 pm Guildford to Redhill		
Loco	U class 2-6-0 No 31797					N class 2-6-0 No 31817			U class 2-6-0 No 31628		
Load	3 coaches, 96 tons tare, 100 tons gross					8 coaches, 236 tons tare, 250 tons gross			3 coaches, 102 tons tare, 105 tons gross		
	miles	sched	mins	secs	speed	mins	secs	speed	mins	secs	speed
Guildford	0.00	0.00	00	00		00	00		00	00	
Shalford Junction	1.19		02	47	32/42	04	45	31/sigs stop*0/36	02	58	32/42
Shalford	1.91	5.30	04	11		06	47		04	24	
	0.00	0.00	00	00		00	00		00	00	
Chilworth and Albury	1.83	4.30	04	13	40	05	05	34	04	09	40
	0.00	0.00	00	00		00	00		00	00	
MP 36¼	2.95		05	30	44/38	07	51	31/22	05	58	40/32
Gomshall and Shere	3.94	7.30	07	17	51	10	14	45	07	54	50
	0.00	0.00	00	00		00	00		00	00	
MP 34	1.25		03	08	37	03	59	26	02	50	40
MP 31	4.25		06	23	64	07	53	67	05	50	70
Dorking Town	4.72		06	49	66	08	18	71	06	36	sigs*
Deepdene	5.43	12.00	08	14		09	37		07	59	
	0.00	0.00	00	00		00	00		00	00	
Betchworth	2.60	5.30	05	23	41	06	02	41	06	15	38/sigs*
	0.00	0.00	00	00		00	00		00	00	
Reigate	2.87	5.30	04	44	52	05	31	48	07	17	51/sigs stop*
	0.00	0.00	00	00		00	00		00	00	
Redhill	1.84	5.00	04	22	41	05	29	36/sigs*	07	05	43/sigs stop*

29 June 1963 N class 31862 leaving Guildford with the 12.37 pm to Reading.

8 July 1963.
N class 31871 near Deepdene with the 11.05 am Reading to Redhill.

to provide alternative entertainment! Runs 1 to 3 are fairly typical and though the running was hardly spectacular timekeeping was generally good enough. I had travelled from East Croydon to Redhill on 24 November in a 6-car train of 2 Bil units on the 1.22 pm which took 13 minutes 10 seconds with a maximum speed of 68mph and thus provided an easy connection into my favourite afternoon train from Redhill, the 2.05 pm, which was headed by N class 2-6-0 No 31817 on the usual three coaches for 105 tons (Run 1).

The schedule up to Reigate was a bit tight bearing in mind the slow start and 1 in 100 climb but the Mogul was worked quite easily throughout, blowing off steam at Gomshall and arriving in Guildford in good time for the return run to Redhill on the 2.55 pm train with another Mogul, this time U class No 31797, also on three lightly loaded coaches (Run 7). Once again the running was fairly typical with good steady hill climbing and a nice spin up to 66mph down Gomshall bank.

On Sundays Dorking Town was closed and many of the other intermediate stations produced little or no trade. We had to wait for a time at Deepdene and were slightly early into Redhill before I caught the 3.45 pm Bil stock train back to East Croydon and home by bus. This pattern was repeated on 22 December with 31866 out (Run 3) and 31628 back (Run 9).

The running was similar but the return run on the 2.55 pm was hindered by signal checks, sufficient for me to miss

2 November 1963. U class 31626 leaving Betchworth with the 11.05 am Reading to Redhill.

the 3.45 pm train back to East Croydon. But it was enlivened by 70mph down the bank after a very good start up the 1 in 96 to the summit from the Gomshall stop, topped at 40mph. On 8 December for a change I caught the 10.46 am from East Croydon to Redhill with 4 Lav units 2936 and 2943 and was able to see 31796 on the 9.03 am from Reading (see photograph) on a very cold, frosty and misty morning, before catching the 11.36 am to Guildford, formed of three coaches of the stock of the Reading train headed by 31806. It was an uneventful run until we ran into dense fog at Chilworth and were held there for thirteen minutes, presumably as fog working was in place, and so arrived at Guildford the same amount late. My return train was the12.55 pm with Mogul 31622 on three coaches and a van which left 12 minutes late but managed to recover 4 minutes to Redhill. This train was interesting as it stopped on the run down Gomshall bank at Coombe Crossing to exchange water cans with the crossing keeper at this remote location, for which

2 November 1963. U class 31628 in the rain soon after leaving Reigate with the 1.35 pm Redhill to Reading.

time was allowed in the schedule. At Redhill I was able to take a shot of U class 31797, one of the engines rebuilt from the K class 2-6-4 tanks, sitting in the sun on my usual train, the 2.05 pm to Guildford, before returning to East Croydon in 2 Hal 2694 with 2 Bil 2053 on the 2.15 pm train which put up a very lively performance reaching 71mph at Coulsdon South, covering the 10.4 miles in 3 seconds under 12 minutes, a time which wouldn't disgrace the electrostar units of today.

The following Sunday, 15 December, the 2.05 pm train was unusually headed by BR Class 4 Mogul 76033 on four coaches (Run 2) and although we left 12 minutes late, no time was recovered and indeed we lost over 2 minutes to Reigate with the engine slipping violently on the 1 in 100 climb out of Redhill. Things then improved with a very respectable climb of Gomshall bank, topped at 39mph, but the lateness was sufficient for me to miss my usual 2.55 pm train back from Guildford. This turned out to be a blessing in disguise as the next train, the 3.57 pm was headed by N Class Mogul 31817 on no less than eight coaches of Maunsell Hastings line stock for a gross weight of 250 tons, a heavy load for this route. Run 8 shows the performance, which was accompanied throughout by lots of noise. Understandably time was lost on some sections and we arrived at Redhill 21 minutes late, not helped by a signal stop at Shalford Junction and being held for 10 minutes at Chilworth. The uphill sections with this load were a real slog – 22mph at the top of the long 1 in 100/96 climb from Chilworth really wasn't bad in the circumstances. Then there was an exhilarating dash down Gomshall bank

8 July 1963. N class 31858 tops Gomshall summit with the 9.45 am Reading to Redhill.

GUILDFORD TO REDHILL

Date	Saturday 26 October 1963				
Run Number	6				
Train	822 am Guildford to Redhill				
Loco	U class 2-6-0 No. 31617				
Load	4 coaches, 130 tons tare, 140 tons gross				
	miles	sched	mins	secs	speed
Guildford	0.00	0.00	00	00	
Shalford Junction	1.19		03	02	27/38
Shalford	1.91	6.30	04	21	
	0.00	0.00	00	00	
Chilworth and Albury	1.83	4.30	03	47	43
	0.00	0.00	00	00	
MP 36¼	2.95		04	58	40/57
Gomshall and Shere	3.94	7.30	06	34	
	0.00	0.00	00	00	
MP 34	1.25		02	50	37
MP 32	3.25		04	58	64
Dorking Town	4.72	8.00	06	53	
	0.00	0.00	00	00	
Deepdene	0.71	2.00	02	08	27
	0.00	0.00	00	00	
Betchworth	2.60	5.30	04	43	42
	0.00	0.00	00	00	
Reigate	2.87	4.30	04	49	53
	0.00	0.00	00	00	
Redhill	1.84	5.00	05	47	41/sigs stop*

to reach 71mph before the Deepdene stop, my highest speed anywhere with a Maunsell N Class.

As I mentioned above sometimes I covered this line as a break from bashing up and down between Waterloo and Woking behind Bulleid Pacifics, and this was quite tempting as the Area Two Day Rovers included the Guildford to Redhill line. This happened on Saturday, 26 October when, having gone down from Waterloo to Woking on the 7.20 am with 34073, I decided that a run on the 10.18 semi-fast from Redhill was required and so I went across to Guildford to catch the 8.22 am train behind U Class Mogul, 31617 on four coaches (Run 6).

This was a good competent performance and enabled me to catch the 10.18 back with N Class 2-6-0 31850 on four coaches

29 June 1963. Manor 4-6-0 7818 *Granville Manor* entering Guildford on the 7.32 am Wolverhampton to Hastings.

for 135 tons (Run 4). The running was enough to keep time and no more, though made a change from the usual stoppers.

Finally for 1963 are two non-stop runs on the Wolverhampton through trains on Saturday, 29 June 1963. The previous year these trains had loaded to as much as thirteen coaches and were hauled by Schools class 4-4-0s but in 1963 Western Region motive power had taken over in the form of Manor Class 4-6-0s. The 7.32 am from Wolverhampton was headed by 7818 *Granville Manor* and left Guildford on time with a load of ten coaches for 365 tons full (Run 5). Overall time was just kept, though that needed some good work from this moderately sized engine on the hills plus a very fast run down Gomshall bank at 73mph.

REDHILL TO GUILDFORD

Date	Saturday 26 October 1963
Run Number	4
Train	1018 am Redhill to Guildford
Loco	N class 2-6-0 No. 31850
Load	4 coaches, 128 tons tare, 135 tons gross

	miles	sched	mins	secs	speed
Redhill	0.00	0.00	00	00	
MP 23¾	1.25		03	50	21/32
Reigate	1.84	3.30	05	33	
	0.00	0.00	00	00	
Betchworth	2.87		04	51	52/47
Deepdene	5.47	8.30	08	16	
	0.00	0.00	00	00	
Dorking Town	0.71	2.30	03	09	19
	0.00	0.00	00	00	
MP 34	3.47		07	35	32/26
Gomshall and Shere	4.72		09	19	55
MP 36¼	5.68		10	31	48
Chilworth and Albury	8.66		13	35	64
Shalford	10.49		15	24	58
Shalford Junction	11.21		16	45	20*/38
Guildford	12.42	19.00	19	06	

8 July 1963. BR class 4 80151 (at that time quite rare) at Gomshall summit with the 10.18 am Redhill to Reading.

29 June 1963 at Redhill. Manor 7824 on the late running 12.20 pm Hastings to Birmingham.

The return was with 7824 *Ilford Manor* also on ten coaches for about 360 tons and once again time was kept with a good climb of Gomshall at 27mph minimum after no more than 60 at Deepdene (Run 10).

In 1964 I had a number of very good runs on the 10.18 am semi-fast from Redhill with BR Class 4 2-6-4 tanks including one where we ran Dorking to Guildford in 16 minutes 31 seconds with 80034. The minimum on Gomshall was 41mph and we dashed into the dip through Gomshall at no less than 70mph and swept over the next summit at 58 before a more normal run down past Chilworth. The reason for this haste was a

GUILDFORD TO REDHILL

Date	29 June 1963				
Run Number	5				
Train	732 am Wolverhampton to Hastings				
Loco	Manor class 4-6-0 No. 7818 *Granville Manor*				
Load	10 coaches, 342 tons tare, 365 tons gross				
Weather	cloudy warm				
	miles	sched	mins	secs	speed
Guildford	0.00	0.00	00	00	
Shalford Junction	1.21		03	19	31
Shalford	1.93		04	28	43
Chilworth and Albury	3.76		07	45	30
MP 36¼	6.69		15	00	21
Gomshall and Shere	7.70		16	47	42
MP 33¾	9.19		19	41	24
Dorking Town	12.41	21.00	23	20	70
Deepdene	13.15		23	56	73
Betchworth	15.76		26	50	42
MP 26¼	16.69		28	11	53
Reigate	18.64		30	42	37/50
Redhill	20.46	34.00	33	51	

8 July 1963. Manor 7808 *Cookham* Manor on the last half mile to Gomshall summit with the 11.20 am Redhill to Guildford.

REDHILL TO GUILDFORD

Date	Saturday 29 June 1963				
Run Number	10				
Train	218 pm Redhill to Guildford				
Loco	Manor class 4-6-0 No 7824 *Ilford Manor*				
Load	10 coaches, 339 tons tare, 360 tons gross				
	miles	sched	mins	secs	speed
Redhill	0.00	0.00	00	00	
MP 23¾	1.25		04	03	21
Reigate	1.84		05	27	29/51
Betchworth	4.71		10	07	47
Deepdene	7.31		13	04	60
Dorking Town	8.02		13	53	48
MP 34	11.49		19	44	27
Gomshall and Shere	12.74		21	49	52
MP 36¼	13.73		23	09	43
Chilworth and Albury	16.68		26	40	65
Shalford	18.51		29	21	sigs 20*/8*
Shalford Junction	19.23		31	02	22/40
Guildford	20.42	36.00	33	49	

13 minute late departure from Redhill and the overall running time including three stops was only just over 33 minutes.

The final day of steam was on Sunday, 3 January 1965 and on that day I travelled down to Redhill by train as I had so many times before and caught the 11.40 am to Guildford which was hauled by BR class 4 Standard 2-6-4 tank No 80151 (now preserved on the Bluebell line just a few miles away) which had four coaches in tow. It was a good run throughout with 61mph before the Betchworth stop and 62 before Deepdene. We then ran non-stop to Chilworth in 13 minutes 14 seconds and arrived in Guildford a couple of minutes

2 November 1963. U class 31628 near Kemps Farm, Betchworth with the 9.45 am Reading to Redhill.

2 November 1963. BR class 4 2-6-0 76034 near Betchworth with the 12.35 pm Redhill to Reading.

8 July 1963. N class 31826 on the final half mile to Gomshall with a freight from Redhill.

18 January 1964. Type 33 No D6595 near Betchworth on a heavy freight for Redhill.

18 January 1964. Hymek D7047 approaching Betchworth with the 11.35 am Redhill to Reading.

18 January 1964. 31831 near Brockham with the 9.03 am Reading to Redhill.

18 January 1964. BR class 4 tank No 80144 near Betchworth with the 11.05 am Reading to Redhill.

18 January 1964. 31801 near Betchworth with the 10.18 am Redhill to Reading.

REDHILL TO GUILDFORD

Date	Sunday 3 January 1965
Run Number	11
Train	1140 am Redhill to Guildford
Loco	BR Class 4 2-6-4 tank No. 80151
Load	4 coaches, 128 tons tare,135 tons gross

	miles	sched	mins	secs	speed
Redhill	0.00	0.00	00	00	
MP 23¾	1.25		03	17	29/sigs stop
Reigate	1.84	3.30	05	56	
	0.00	0.00	00	00	
Betchworth	2.87	5.30	04	34	44/61
	0.00	0.00	00	00	
Deepdene	2.60	4.30	03	56	62
	0.00	0.00	00	00	
Dorking Town	0.71		01	57	34
MP 34	4.18		07	07	45
Gomshall and Shere	5.43		08	28	64
MP 36¼	6.42		09	39	48/61
Chilworth and Albury	9.37	15.00	13	14	
	0.00	0.00	00	00	
Shalford	1.83	4.30	03	33	48 max
	0.00	0.00	00	00	
Shalford Junction	0.72		02	03	48 max
Guildford	1.91	4.30	04	26	

late after taking water at Shalford; a most unusual occurrence! Full details are shown in Log 11. At Guildford I noted USA tank No 30072, Q1 0-6-0 No 33018 and U class 2-6-0 No 31620 before catching the 1.55 pm train back to Redhill behind N class No 31816 also on four coaches, which produced an average run after leaving 12 minutes late to arrive just 6 late with no higher speed than 56mph down Gomshall bank. The return to Guildford was on the 2.05 pm train with U class No 31809 and this also left late at 2.09 pm. With three coaches we did all that was needed with a minimum of 37mph on Gomshall bank and a maximum speed of 60 through Gomshall to arrive in Guildford on time.

Our little group then awaited the

18 January 1964. 31831 near Betchworth with the 12.35 pm Redhill to Reading.

arrival of the 2.55 pm to Redhill which was to be my last run on this line with steam until the return to steam era. Unusually the train was headed by BR class 4 2-6-0 No 76059 and we had a heavy load of seven coaches of around 240 tons full. Our driver, by the name of Soil, was obviously intent on recovering as much as possible of the thirteen minute late start and so the climbs were attacked with much vigour and noise and the minimum past Shere was an excellent and sustained 34mph. The footplate crew then let fly to reach no less than 74mph down to the Deepdene stop, my highest recorded speed on this line. We continued well to arrive in Redhill just 5 minutes late having regained 8 minutes. What a splendid run to sign off steam with on one of my favourite lines.

GUILDFORD TO REDHILL

Date	Sunday 3 January 1965
Run Number	12
Train	255 pm Guildford to Redhill
Loco	BR Class 4 2-6-0 No. 76059
Load	7 coaches, 228 tons tare, 240 tons gross
Driver	J Soil

	miles	sched	mins	secs	speed
Guildford	0.00	0.00	00	00	
Shalford Junction	1.19		02	54	36/47
Shalford	1.91	6.30	04	12	
	0.00	0.00	00	00	
Chilworth and Albury	1.83	4.30	04	16	37
	0.00	0.00	00	00	
MP 36¼	2.95		06	17	34
Gomshall and Shere	3.94		07	32	53½
MP 34	5.19		09	19	41
MP 31	8.19		12	24	74
Dorking Town	8.66		12	50	67½
Deepdene	9.37	15.00	13	48	
	0.00	0.00	00	00	
Betchworth	2.60	5.30	05	28	37½
	0.00	0.00	00	00	
Reigate	2.87	5.30	05	23	47½
	0.00	0.00	00	00	
Redhill	1.84	4.00	04	15	43

Chapter Eight

South Western Engineering Works

This set of pictures is interesting as they show how engineering works were usually carried out on main lines over fifty years ago, in this case on 24 March 1963 in the Wimbledon area of South West London. The priority then was to try to keep as far as possible to the normal service and it was very rare for buses to be substituted. Of course work today is carried out on a grand scale using large machinery which is often out of gauge and blocks adjoining tracks. Also the split of functions now encourages the easy option of line closures, compared to when there was one railway. Looking at these images it seems that just as many people are required trackside now as was the case then, despite greater mechanisation now. The image captions tell the tale of that calm, mild Sunday morning over fifty years ago.

4 EPB Unit No 5120 comes off the line from Sutton via Wimbledon Chase with a stopping train to London, Waterloo. In the background Q1 class 0-6-0 No 33032 stands on the up fast line with a train of wagons from which the track gang are discharging ballast onto the track base of the down main line from which the old track has been removed. Nearer to the engine is a row of ballast wagons, suggesting that maybe these contain the new ballast and the men are removing the old. Nearer to the camera is the new track waiting to be laid. Notice how close some of the workers are to the down slow line which was still in full use.

Work continues as a few minutes later Bulleid 'BB' class 4-6-2 No.34060 *25 Squadron* passes on the up slow line with the Sundays only 7.10 am Yeovil Town to Waterloo service which would have reversed at Yeovil Junction. Two lookout men can just be seen on the left near to Wimbledon C signal box, dating from 1929.

As the up Yeovil train passed I turned round to see a down steam hauled train approaching and this proved to be the 10.30 am Waterloo to Bournemouth West and Weymouth headed by Bulleid Merchant Navy class Pacific No 35018 *British India Line*. Running on the down slow line it was about to pass the scene of the relaying of the down fast line with the gangers and lookout men close to the running line and not a hi-viz jacket in sight!

For the next two shots I cycled to a location just west of Raynes Park near to the Carter's Seed factory. Here we see another Q1 class 0-6-0 Coffee Pot No 33027 on a long train of wagons, possibly from the site of the track works at Wimbledon.

Shortly afterwards along came Bulleid unrebuilt BB class 4-6-2 No 34073 *249 Squadron* on the 11 am Waterloo to Exeter carrying portions for Plymouth and Ilfracombe. On Sundays this train was semi-fast calling at all principal stations as far as Exeter as opposed to weekdays when it called only at Salisbury and Sidmouth Junction before Exeter. Unusually it's not Merchant Navy hauled, but instead has a Nine Elms light Pacific in charge.

Back to Wimbledon now to see that 33032 had moved the now empty ballast wagons up towards Waterloo suggesting progress with the track laying. In the background is the footpath where I spent many happy hours photographing the passing steam hauled trains from 1961 until the end of steam in 1967.

Finally a nice shot of BR Standard class 5 4-6-0 No 73085 on the 11.30 am Waterloo to Bournemouth West and Weymouth passing 33032 still standing on the up fast line with its wagons, the crew of which were about to wave to the driver of the Class 5 on the down slow. If you were travelling on the 11.30 am down you would be able to enjoy the ambience of Bournemouth Central station for no less than 41 minutes as this portion of the train waited for the arrival at 2.40 pm of the 12.30 pm Bournemouth Belle all-Pullman car train from Waterloo. No 73085 was a Nine Elms engine at that time but during the week the 11.30 down would normally be an Eastleigh Bulleid light Pacific.

Chapter Nine

A Wet Day on Upwey Bank – Saturday, 6 July 1963

6 July 1963. 34093 *Saunton* south of Upwey Wishing Well Halt.

"The gradients from Weymouth are fearsome though not prolonged"

6 July 1963. 73080 *Merlin* and 73087 *Linette* passing the Upwey down distant signal with the 1.30 pm Weymouth to Waterloo.

I had few clear objectives for my 1963 Southern Region Rail Rover and indeed most of the week was spent bashing Merchant Navy class Pacifics on the Atlantic Coast Express and Bournemouth 2-hour trains. I had chosen a good week for the down ACE as driver Charlie Hopgood from Salisbury shed turned in consistently good performances every day with net or actual times to Salisbury being entirely within the narrow range of 77 to 79 minutes for the 83.7 miles with no more than very modest excesses over the 85mph speed limit. Typical of the top link at Salisbury shed at that time. The up ACE also produced some good performances with driver Bert Cambray, also of Salisbury shed, the best being with 35009 on Friday, 5 July when we kept the 80 minute schedule despite a long relaying slack near Hurstbourne, leaving a net time of under 75 minutes.

4924 *Eydon Hall* leaving Bournemouth Central with the 8.48 am New Milton to Swansea.

73089 *Maid of Astolat* south of Upwey Wishing Well Halt on the 9.24 am Waterloo to Weymouth.

However I did know what I wanted to do for the last day of the rover, which was to spend a summer Saturday on Upwey Bank mainly for the purpose of photographing heavy trains climbing the 1 in 50 gradient. Saturday, 6 July would be well into the summer timetable which that year ran from 17 June until 8 September.

In addition to the Channel Islands Boat train which always loaded to at least ten coaches and would be likely to be running with at least one relief train, some of the more popular services to Waterloo would be running as a complete train through from Weymouth, with a separate train from Bournemouth West, instead of the normal weekday practice of portions from each joining at Bournemouth Central. There was also a Channel Islands Boat train connection to Cardiff which was still booked to be a heavy steam hauled train. So I was looking forward to plenty of action with a good mixture of motive power and most uphill trains banked or double-headed. It was also to be the last summer of the Great Western County class 4-6-0s working through to Weymouth, although many trains from the Westbury route were by then Diesel Mechanical Multiple units. On the Southern section there were a few non-steam incursions, with Diesel Electric Multiple units on most of the stopping trains to and from Eastleigh.

My day started very early on the 4.40 am from Elmers End to Waterloo with 4EPB units, where, after walking across from the Eastern side, I boarded the 5.40 am semi-fast train to Bournemouth and Weymouth.

It was a gloomy morning so typical of that very poor summer and instead of the expected Bulleid Pacific my train was headed by BR class 5 4-6-0 No 73087. Out of Waterloo this was quite a heavy train, comprising five passenger coaches and seven vans conveying mail.

One van would be dropped at Woking and another at Basingstoke, reducing our

1006 *County of Cornwall* struggles past Upwey and Broadwey station with the 4.15 pm Weymouth Quay to Cardiff.

73116 *Iseult* and 73017 pass Upwey and Broadwey station with the 3.50 pm Weymouth to Waterloo.

34018 *Axminster* passing Upwey and Broadwey station with the 8.15 am Waterloo to Weymouth Quay.

gross load from about 350 tons to 280 tons after Basingstoke. The '5' did quite well on a fairly easy schedule which allowed for mail to be unloaded en route, the maximum speed for the trip being 76mph between the Micheldever and Winchester stops. Arrival at Bournemouth was on time and I decided to break my journey here to take a few photos and consider whether it was worth continuing as the rain was now falling steadily.

At Bournemouth the variety of a summer Saturday was evident, with 6929 *Whorlton Hall* noted on the 9.10 am Bournemouth West to Derby (Friargate), 4924 *Eydon Hall* on the 8.48 am New Milton to Swansea and 34105 *Swanage* on the 9.28 am Bournemouth West to Manchester and Liverpool. This latter train would have operated via the Somerset and Dorset Joint line until the end of the previous summer. The New Milton train was routed from Bournemouth via Wimborne, Salisbury and Westbury, though why it started at New Milton rather than Bournemouth is not known – maybe to do with stock workings and platform occupation at Bournemouth which was a busy place at that time on a summer Saturday morning. I could have done worse than catch this train to Salisbury as at that time I had not covered the track between Poole and Salisbury.

However I contented myself with a shot of the *Hall* leaving in the rain and stuck to my plan by joining the 7.45 am from Waterloo. It rolled in on time behind 34098 *Templecombe*, an Eastleigh engine, and deposited me in Weymouth just after 11 am. My lineside photographic pass was for Dorchester to Weymouth exclusive, but did not allow access to depots or tunnels so I planned to concentrate on the section from south of Upwey and Broadwey station to Upwey Wishing Well Halt, having walked in the rain past Radipole to gain access to the lineside from an overbridge.

The line from Dorchester to Weymouth was originally opened by the Great Western Railway in 1857 as the southern section of the line from Castle Cary via Yeovil. The London and South Western Railway also operated services over this section of line via Dorchester South. Upwey Wishing Well Halt was opened in 1905 and closed in 1957 although the platforms remained at the time of my visit. Upwey and Broadwey station was opened in 1871 as Upwey, being renamed Upwey Junction in 1886 when the line to Abbotsbury opened. When this branch closed to passengers in 1952 the station was again renamed, this time to Upwey and Broadwey. Finally in 1980 it was renamed back to the original Upwey. Has any station in the UK been renamed more? At the time of my visit the points and a short stretch of track for the Abbotsbury branch as far as Upwey still existed as freight had only been withdrawn on 1 January 1962. Radipole Halt was opened by the GWR in 1905, renamed Radipole in 1969 and closed in 1984. Mileposts are on the west (up) side of the line in keeping with normal Great Western practice and the route mileage is from Paddington via Westbury, Weymouth being 168 miles 57 chains and Upwey 166 miles and 66 chains. Weymouth is 142 miles 64 chains from Waterloo via Bournemouth.

The gradients from Weymouth are fearsome though not prolonged. After a short level stretch the line climbs at 1 in 187 to the overbridge just past the site of Radipole Halt, then steepens to 1 in 74 until the north end of Upwey station before the mile and a quarter of 1 in 50 to

73022 with a heavy freight, banked by 73041, climbing past the closed Upwey Wishing Well Halt.

1028 *County of Warwick* south of Bincombe tunnel with the 11.52 am Westbury to Weymouth.

6971 *Athelhampton Hall* south of Upwey station with the 7.05 am Birmingham Snow Hill to Weymouth service.

34031 *Torrington* with the 8.30 am Waterloo to Weymouth.

the entrance to Bincombe tunnel (819 yards) where it eases slightly to 1 in 52 to the summit at the north end, just over four and a quarter miles from Weymouth. In steam days trains were limited to seven coaches with one engine; the normal maximum train length was eleven coaches with a pilot or, more usually, a banking engine. It is extraordinary to think that 34067 *Tangmere* took eleven coaches unaided from Weymouth on 9 July 2009 after the class 37 diesel banking engine had failed. All credit to driver Pete Roberts, fireman John Shaw and that magnificent Bulleid pacific which even coped with a slip just before the entrance to the tunnel but still managed to top the climb at a very creditable 15mph. On my return from Weymouth on 6 July

UPWEY BANK - Saturday 6 July 1963

Down trains

Train	Time	Engine	Number	Notes
925 am Westbury to Weymouth	1130 am	DMMU		
815 am Waterloo to Weymouth Quay	1135 am	WC 4-6-2	34018	On time
705 am Birmingham Snow Hill to Weymouth	1205 pm	Modified Hall 4-6-2	6971	20 late
830 am Waterloo to Weymouth	1215 pm	WC 4-6-2	34031	10 late
1012 am Eastleigh to Weymouth	1220 pm	DEMU	1110	
943 am Bristol Temple Meads to Weymouth	1225 pm	County 4-6-0	1006	5 coaches
1155 am Yeovil Pen Mill to Weymouth	100 pm	DMMU		
924 am Waterloo to Weymouth	105 pm	BR Standard '5'	73089	11 coaches
925 am Wimbledon to Weymouth	135 pm	WC 4-6-2	34093	9 coaches
1152 am Westbury to Weymouth	140 pm	County 4-6-0	1028	15 late
1247 pm Westbury to Weymouth	215 pm	DMMU		
1030 am Waterloo to Weymouth	220 pm	BB 4-6-2	34090	30 late
1155 am Eastleigh to Weymouth	230 pm	DEMU	1310	
200 pm Yeovil Pen Mill to Weymouth	300 pm	DMMU		
1122 am Waterloo to Weymouth	315 pm	BR Standard '5'	73112	30 late
1235 pm Waterloo to Weymouth	410 pm	WC 4-6-2	34107	25 late
105 pm Bristol Temple Meads to Weymouth	420 pm	BR Standard '5'	73020	On time
205 pm Eastleigh to Weymouth	430 pm	BR Standard '5'	73xxx	On time
430 pm Maiden Newton to Weymouth	500 pm	DMMU		
1110 am Wolverhampton Low Level to Weymouth	530 pm	Hall 4-6-0	4931	10 coaches

73042 leaving Upwey and Broadwey station with the 12.10 pm Weymouth to Bournemouth Central.

34098 *Templecombe*, banked by 73041, climbs the 1 in 50 with the 3.15 pm Weymouth to Waterloo relief.

34107 *Blandford Forum* passing Upwey and Broadwey with the 12.35 pm Waterloo to Weymouth.

34101 *Hartland* approaching Upwey and Broadwey station with the 3.30 pm Weymouth Quay to Waterloo.

UPWEY BANK - Saturday 6 July 1963

Up trains

Train	Engine	Number	Notes
1125 am Weymouth to Waterloo	BB 4-6-2	34090	11 coaches. Banked by 0-6-0 Pannier tank No 4624
1140 am Weymouth to Yeovil Pen Mill	DMMU		
1210 pm Weymouth to Bournemouth Central	BR Standard '5' 4-6-0	73042	5 coaches
1253 pm Weymouth to Bristol	?	?	
100 pm Weymouth to Yeovil Pen Mill	DMMU		
130 pm Weymouth to Waterloo	BR Standard '5' 4-6-0	73080+73087	11 coaches. Double headed
150 pm Weymouth to Cardiff	DMMU		
Freight at 225 pm	BR Standard '5' 4-6-0	73022	Banked by BR Standard '5' 4-6-0 No 73041
230 pm Weymouth to Eastleigh	DEMU	1110	
240 pm Weymouth to Bristol	DMMU		
300 pm Weymouth Quay to Waterloo	WC 4-6-2	34031	Banked by BR Standard '4' 2-6-0 No 76057
315 pm Relief Weymouth to Waterloo	WC 4-6-2	34098	11 coaches. Banked by BR Standard '5' 4-6-0 No 73041
330 pm Weymouth to Southampton Central	DEMU	1310	
338 pm Weymouth to Maiden Newton	DMMU		
330 pm Weymouth Quay to Waterloo	WC 4-6-2	34101	11 coaches. Banked by BR Standard '4' 2-6-0 No 76057
350 pm Weymouth to Waterloo	BR Standard '5' 4-6-0	73116+73017	Double headed
415 pm Weymouth Quay to Cardiff	County class 4-6-0	1006	11 coaches. Banked by BR Standard '5' 4-6-0 No 73041
442 pm Weymouth to Bournemouth	BB 4-6-2	34090	
535 pm Weymouth to Waterloo	BR Standard '5' 4-6-0	73112	5 coaches

73112 *Morgan Le Fay* just south of Bincombe tunnel with the 11.22 am Waterloo to Weymouth.

1963 we were doing the same speed at the top with BR class 5 4-6-0 73112 with just five coaches!

The photographs and tables show the day's proceedings with one or two surprises evident, notably the appearance of Exmouth Junction Bulleid light Pacific 34107 *Blandford Forum* on the 12.35 pm from Waterloo. This engine had obviously been purloined by Nine Elms the week before as I had seen it at Southampton on Thursday, 4 July working the 10.50 am Bournemouth West to Newcastle train which it would have taken as far as Oxford.

My quest to see the GWR County Class 4-6-0s was fulfilled and I was also more than pleased with the extra afternoon train from Weymouth to Waterloo plus the extent of banking, undertaken mainly by BR Standard class 5 4-6-0 73041 and Class 4 2-6-0 76057, making quite a procession in the rain and cold conditions. The ex GWR 0-6-0 Pannier tank 4624, resident at Weymouth, only put in one appearance, banking the 11.25 am to Waterloo. There were also two trains double-headed, the pilot engines of which (73080 and 73116) didn't return down the bank, probably because they

UPWEY BANK - Saturday 6 July 1963

Shed Allocations of engines

1006	Bristol	(Bath Road)
1028	Bristol	(Bath Road)
4624	Weymouth	(Radipole)
4931	Cardiff	(Canton)
6971	Tyseley	
34018	Nine Elms	
34031	Nine Elms	
34090	Nine Elms	
34093	Nine Elms	
34098	Eastleigh	
34101	Nine Elms	
34107	Exmouth Junction	
73017	Weymouth	(Radipole)
73020	Weymouth	(Radipole)
73022	Weymouth	(Radipole)
73041	Weymouth	(Radipole)
73042	Weymouth	(Radipole)
73080	Weymouth	(Radipole)
73087	Nine Elms	
73089	Nine Elms	
73112	Nine Elms	
73116	Nine Elms	
76057	Weymouth	(Radipole)

6 July 1963. 34031 *Torrington* at the head of the 3 pm Weymouth Quay to Waterloo.

6 July 1963. 76057 banking the 3 pm Weymouth Quay to Waterloo train.

73080 *Merlin* pilots 73087 *Linette* on the 1.30 pm Weymouth to Waterloo.

34090 *Sir Eustace Missenden, Southern* Railway just south of Bincombe tunnel with the 10.30 am Waterloo to Weymouth.

were both Nine Elms engines. The 11.25 am up train was hauled by 34090 *Sir Eustace Missenden* which must have had a lightning turnaround at Bournemouth as it returned on the 10.30 am from Waterloo running about half an hour late. Bournemouth shed must have been very short of motive power that day. The day's work for this engine still wasn't finished as it worked back again on the 4.42 pm to Bournemouth.

By the end of the day I was thoroughly soaked by the rain but reasonably happy with my tally of 24 steam hauled trains on Upwey bank and the 23 different engines seen, from 6 different sheds. I was looking forward to the return run to Waterloo behind the booked Bulleid light Pacific, but BR Standard Class 73112 turned up on the 5.35 pm. However it gave a good account of itself on five coaches as far as Bournemouth and eleven for 400 tons from there, keeping time on the extended summer Saturday schedule for this train. I would have arrived home at about 9.30 pm no doubt to a reheated dinner and a cup of tea.

Chapter Ten

South West London Steam – November 1963

The Wimbledon-Raynes Park-New Malden area was much visited in the days of steam as it was easily reached by bicycle from my home in Shirley, near Croydon. There were (and still are) a number of good locations from which to watch and photograph trains and in the autumn of 1963 all trains on the main lines to Bournemouth and Salisbury were still steam worked, even if the variety of the year before was much diminished by the cull of December 1962. I had moved on from my first 35mm camera, an East German Franka of dubious quality, and was using a second-hand Agifold 6x6 folding camera which could produce reasonable results if the film stock was developed properly, although this wasn't always the case! So here is a selection of images from November 1963 on my favourite piece of railway at that time.

This was taken on Sunday, 3 November 1963 from the bridge over the South Western main line just on the London side of New Malden station. Urie S15 4-6-0 No 30512, allocated to Feltham shed, was working the 9-coach Locomotive Club of Great Britain 'Hayling Island Farewell' special to commemorate the closure of the Hayling Island branch that day. The train had left Waterloo at 9.44 am and was routed via the Mid Hants line and Winchester to Portsmouth, Havant and Hayling Island, returning via the Arun Valley line to Victoria after a side trip to Lavant from Chichester. Engines used that day were 30512, 30531, 30543, 31791, 32636, 32670 and 34088, an incredible variety of motive power even then.

ABOVE: About 45 minutes later, at the same location as 30512, rebuilt Merchant Navy class pacific 35020 *Bibby Line* was photographed working the 10.30 am Waterloo to Bournemouth and Weymouth. This train was worked by a Nine Elms top link driver and firemen who would take the train as far as Bournemouth, before returning later in the day with the same engine. At that time there were no Merchant Navy class engines allocated to Weymouth so another engine, probably a Bulleid light Pacific, would work the train forward from Bournemouth. This train was an easier proposition on Sundays than weekdays, as the schedule was eleven minutes longer to Bournemouth with just the one extra stop at Winchester as well as Southampton.

OPPOSITE PAGE:
TOP: Just down the road at Raynes Park and in the shadow of the Kingston Bypass was a nice open location next to the erstwhile Carter's Seed factory. Shots could be taken of trains going both ways and this image taken on Saturday, 16 November 1963 shows BR class 5 4-6-0 No 73046 working the 9.54 am Waterloo to Basingstoke local train, which was fast to Woking, booked in 31 minutes for the 24.3 miles. This engine had an interesting history. It was delivered new to Leicester (LMS) in 1955 and then transferred to Sheffield (Millhouses) in 1959 where it stayed until 1962 when it went to Rotherham until 1963 when it had its final move to Nine Elms. Thus it differed from the main batch of class 5s on the Southern (73080-73089 and 73110-73119) which had been there since 1959.

LOWER: After seeing the Class 5 and 34046 on an up local train from Basingstoke, I moved to the footpath on the north side of the line to the west of Wimbledon station for the rest of the morning. First came 35024 on the up Royal Wessex and then 34018 *Axminster* photographed here working the 10.30 am Waterloo to Bournemouth. Even with eleven MK 1 and Bulleid coaches, the fairly tight 2-hour schedule to Bournemouth would have presented no problems to the Nine Elms crew. This train was booked to be hauled by one of the larger Merchant Navy class Pacifics but most Nine Elms drivers would have coped easily unlike certain drivers from other depots, notably Bournemouth, who would automatically have used the provision of a light Pacific as good enough reason to lose time, sometimes even announcing this in advance of the run! 34018 was at Nine Elms from 1951 until its withdrawal in 1967, except for a brief spell at Eastleigh in 1964/65. It was rebuilt in 1958 and lasted right to the end of steam on 9 July 1967, having accumulated nearly a million miles.

ABOVE: Soon after 34018 had passed came a filthy 34104 *Bere Alston* on that misty Saturday, 16 November 1963 working the 8.46 am Salisbury to Waterloo semi-fast service, due at Waterloo at 11.16 am. This was an Eastleigh engine at that time having started life at Stewarts Lane and ending at Nine Elms where it lasted almost to the end of steam. In the 1960s and until the previous year this train had usually been a Salisbury King Arthur turn, the engine working home on the 2.54 pm semi-fast from Waterloo. For many months the usual engine was 30451 which on 28 April that year gave me a fine run up from Woking with a maximum speed of 76mph. In contrast to this shabby engine, without its crest, Salisbury shed always kept their engines in immaculate condition and this tradition continues today with the class 159 diesel units. On the left is Wimbledon 'C' box and the line to Sutton.

OPPOSITE PAGE:

TOP: Soon after the up Salisbury semi-fast had passed, 35020 *Bibby Line* appeared on the 13-coach 11 am ex Waterloo Atlantic Coast Express. This heavily loaded train of around 470 tons on that misty 16 November had the fastest scheduled times for steam that had ever existed on the Southern, not known for its progressive approach to such things. The 83.7 miles to Salisbury were allowed just 80 minutes and the 75.9 miles on over the switchback route to Exmouth Junction 75 minutes. I had some very fine runs on this train, with many times of around 76 minutes to Salisbury and below 70 minutes twice on to Exmouth Junction. This train was timed to reach Exeter in 2 minutes less than 3 hours and carried portions for Ilfracombe and Padstow at this time of year. Once the line west of Salisbury had passed to the Western Region in 1964 this train's days were numbered as the Western gradually tried to strangle and close the line; it last ran on 5 September 1964. Fortunately the line survives and prospers today with the remaining singled sections inhibiting further growth.

LOWER: One week later on Saturday, 23 November on a fine afternoon, I spent a couple of hours on the platforms at Wimbledon photographing steam on the main line. 35018 *British India* Line was working the 3 pm Waterloo to Exeter. This train was semi-fast with the first stop at Basingstoke. It carried through coaches to Plymouth and Ilfracombe, both reached in time for supper. In the middle of the picture is Wimbledon 'A' signal box. On the extreme left are the semaphore signals for the District Line/joint Southern line to East Putney and on the right signals on the line from Streatham. 35018 was delivered new to Nine Elms in 1945 and spent its whole life there, running a total of 956,500 miles before an early withdrawal in August 1964. It was the first Merchant Navy class pacific to be rebuilt in February 1956.

Chapter Eleven

Steam Around London

5016 *Montgomery Castle* heading the 2.55 pm to Swansea and Milford Haven at Paddington on 29 October 1961.

"If we used the Circle Line from Victoria we could access the delights of Paddington, Kings Cross and Euston"

This chapter is unashamedly a collection of some of my favourite images taken entirely in the period 1960 to 1963 and includes some of my earliest colour shots, fortunately taken on Kodak 6x9 cm film with my Kodak folding camera. Until I got married in 1968 I lived in the South London area, first at St Mary Cray, then Bromley and finally at Shirley, near Croydon. It was when we moved to Bromley that I started to explore the nearby locations for trainspotting purposes, the natural progression being the acquisition of the inevitable Brownie 127 camera which started my long standing hobby of railway photography, which continues to this day. Bromley South and Grove Park were natural spots and I managed to accumulate a lot of photos from both places, many of dubious quality as I mistakenly thought that moving up from the basic Brownie to a Kodak folding camera with a top shutter speed of a hundred and twenty fifth of a second would guarantee good results.

Nevertheless I managed to record the end of main line steam on South Eastern lines even including the occasional foray by train to Victoria. The *Golden Arrow* featured high on my agenda and was always hauled by a beautifully turned out Stewarts Lane Bulleid light Pacific in the

34100 *Appledore* in Bickley cutting on the down Golden Arrow on 7 June 1961.

H class 31550 brings the ECS of a boat train into Platform 2 at Victoria on 11 March 1961.

31507 on the 7.24 am London Bridge to Ramsgate approaching Elmstead Woods tunnel in the last week of steam, June 1961.

In June 1961, in the last week of steam, 34067 *Tangmere* passing Bromley South with an up boat train.

34101 *Hartland* passing Bromley South on an up boat train in May 1961.

Spring and early Summer of 1961, usually No 34100 *Appledore*, or 34101 *Hartland*. Other trains of particular interest were the 9.10 am Charing Cross to Ramsgate and the unique 7.24 am London Bridge to Ramsgate, which was nearly always headed by a Maunsell E1, D1 or L1 4-4-0, though I remember once seeing a C Class 0-6-0 deputising. I even found the money for a couple of runs on this train.

Before that my younger brother and I had found our way by train from Bromley North to London Bridge and then, by walking, to the cab road at Liverpool Street, though I didn't record anything of those days and it wasn't until after the end of South Eastern steam that I bagged a couple of shots there. Much more appealing was the South Western main line at Wimbledon, reached by a short

ORPINGTON TO ASHFORD

Date	4 January 1961
Train	724 am London Bridge to Ramsgate
Loco	D1 Class 4-4-0 No. 31489
Load	4 coaches and 3 vans, 215 tons
Timed by	Don Benn
Weather	cold and wet

	miles	sched	mins	secs	speed
Orpington	0.00	0.00	00	00	
Chelsfield	1.50		04	00	32
Knockholt	2.74		06	15	38
Dunton Green	6.76		11	00	66
Sevenoaks	8.30	14.00	13	00	
	0.00	0.00	00	00	
Hildenborough	4.91		09	00	60/sigs stop 0*
Tonbridge	7.41	12.00	16	00	
	0.00	0.00	00	00	
Paddock Wood	5.29		08	00	54
Marden	9.86		13	00	57
Staplehurst	12.34		15	15	68
Headcorn	15.73		18	15	72
Pluckley	20.91		22	45	65/68
Chart Siding	24.47		26	15	60/sigs 20*
Ashford	26.59	32.00	30	15	

net time 28½ mins
timed to nearest quarter minute

26 September 1961. 30796 *Sir Dodinas le Savage* approaching Wimbledon with the 8.46 am Salisbury to Waterloo.

34077 passing Bromley South on a down boat train, March 1961.

The crew of 34025 look for the photographer as the 9.10 am Charing Cross to Ramsgate storms to Elmstead Woods tunnel in June 1961.

29 September 1961. 34091 *Weymouth* passing Clapham Junction with the 2.54 pm Waterloo to Basingstoke.

60518 *Tehran* backs out of Kings Cross, August 1960.

6942 *Eshton Hall* backs into Paddington, October 1960.

60014 *Silver Link* at Kings Cross on 19 September 1961.

B1 class 61149 with L1 67703 and D6711 at Liverpool Street, July 1961.

70006 *Robert Burns* stands at Liverpool Street in the rain with a down train in July 1961.

60110 *Robert the Devil* leaving Kings Cross with a down express on 19 September 1961.

90428 passing Hatfield with an up freight, 27 October 1962.

60500 *Edward Thompson* and 60136 *Alcazar* at Kings Cross on 19 September 1961.

cycle ride. Many hours were spent on the footbridges and footpath there, sometimes even straying by train to Clapham Junction where some half decent colour shots were obtained, fortunately using the archival quality Kodak negative film.

By September 1961 I had bought a cheap East German Franka 35mm camera and this was used with some success for about a year, during which time my brother and I had discovered that if we used the Circle Line from Victoria we could access the delights of Paddington, Kings Cross and Euston, the first two seeing many visits as steam was still there in good quantity until around mid 1963.

As Chapter Five shows, the South Western main line held most of my attention in 1962, but there were also trips to the Sussex area, with Groombridge being within cycling distance and offering the chance to photograph frequent steam hauled trains. Even the Brighton main line had its attractions and one train in particular held a fascination for me: the 5.25 pm London Bridge to Reading via Redhill, which was booked to be hauled by a Brighton based Schools Class 4-4-0.

6002 *King William IV* heading a van train at Paddington on 29 October 1961.

60056 *Centenary* passing Hatfield with an up freight, 27 October 1962.

6002 leaving Paddington on 29 October 1961 with a down afternoon van train.

6989 *Wightwick Hall* at Paddington after arrival with the 9.50 am from Worcester on 29 October 1961.

I got many shots of this train including some taken in the depth of winter using flash, though these weren't too successful. The scenic Redhill to Guildford line also had many visits, and this is covered in Chapter Seven.

From April 1963 I was using an Agifold 6x6 camera and this took me through to the end of steam. It could generally be relied on provided I developed the films properly. It took me into a new era of chasing steam out of Kings Cross, until its demise in June 1963, and also on the Great Western main line; also Sussex for remaining steam, another little gem there being the Three Bridges to East Grinstead line, operated by H and M7 Class 0-4-4 tanks, including the now preserved 31263; and the Oxted lines weren't neglected either.

But if 1962 was the summer for steam out of Waterloo, many Saturdays in the poor summer of 1963 were spent at locations on the Kenton to Bushey section of the line out of Euston where the number of steam hauled trains rivalled that still seen out of Waterloo. The latter had lost its attraction a bit as the end of 1962 had seen the withdrawal of the remaining King Arthurs, Schools and Lord Nelsons. When I think back now at the distances and number of places I cycled to I am amazed that I managed it all without incident, though of course road traffic then was much lighter than now, as was the pace of life generally.

There are some familiar numbers amongst the locomotives pictured in this chapter, as some have been preserved and can still be seen working on the main line or preserved lines today, or being overhauled or restored to working order.

8458 shunting stock for a van train at Paddington on 29 October 1961.

20 July 1963, Kenton. 46237 *City of Bristol* on the 11.40 ex Euston Lakes Express.

18 September 1960. 34010 *Sidmouth* at Waterloo with the 8.35 am to Bournemouth.

27 July 1963. 45529 *Stephenson* and 46252 *City of Leicester* on shed at Camden 7.10 am.

At 4.39 pm on Saturday, 20 July 1963 44786 passes South Kenton with a down freight.

45156 *Ayrshire Yeomanry* near Kenton on a down freight on 9 July 1963.

27 July 1963. 45529 *Stephenson* on the 1.05pm Llandudno to Euston at Harrow.

15 June 1963. 60046 *Diamond Jubilee* passing Oakleigh Park on the 7.18 am Grantham to Kings Cross.

15 June 1963. 60017 *Silver Fox* at Oakleigh Park with the 9 am from Kings Cross to York.

V2 60912 and A3 60112 *St Simon* emerge from Oakleigh Park tunnel going north, to new homes.

2 June 1963, Coulsdon North. 45434 down Midland Excursion.

4 June 1962. 30911 *Dover* near South Croydon with the 5.25 pm London Bridge to Reading via Redhill.

48517 on a freight from Willesden near Clapham Junction on 5 July 1963, seen from a 4EPB unit.

3 September 1963. 76043 at Northwick Park on an up freight.

9 June 1963. 46245 leaving Oakleigh Park tunnel with the 9.15 am Kings Cross to Doncaster HCRS special.

26 May 1963. 31263 enters Grange Road with the 12.40 pm East Grinstead to Three Bridges.

2 June 1962. 31543 near Groombridge with the 11am Tunbridge Wells to Oxted.

7029 *Clun Castle* passing West Ealing on the 9.15 am Paddington to Hereford and Worcester on 21 June 1963.

26 May 1963. 31263 entering Rowfant with the 12.08 pm Three Bridges to East Grinstead.

7903 *Foremarke Hall* passing West Ealing with a freight for the Greenford branch on 21 June 1963.

6986 *Rydal Hall* on a down van train at Iver on 21 June 1963.

7002 *Devizes Castle* near Slough with the 6.55 am Cheltenham Spa to Paddington on 22 June 1963.

6128 on a down freight at Iver on 21 June 1963.

Chapter Twelve

Duchess To Rugby

Another view of 46228 restarting the 11.25 am Euston to Llandudno from the signal stop at Kensal Green. (Photo John Tiley)

"By 1964, their last year, they were becoming rare on anything out of Euston"

Being a Southern man born and bred I was late coming to the London Midland steam scene and it was 1963 before this 18-year-old took any serious notice of the large amount of steam still working out of Euston. Most of the summer Saturdays that year were spent on the LM main line at various locations between Euston and Watford Junction, travelling by bicycle from my south London home, and with two late summer forays to Crewe and the north Wales coast line by rail. The Duchess class Pacifics, already quite scarce, were my favourites and I would be pleased if I saw more than three or four in a day.

By 1964, their last year, they were becoming rare on anything out of Euston,

46228 *Duchess of Rutland* restarts the 11.25 am Euston to Llandudno from a signal stop at Kensal Green. (Photo John Tiley)

30 July 1963. No. 46233 *Duchess of Sutherland* passing Headstone Lane with the 11 am Holyhead to Euston.

being displaced by Britannias and class 4 D200 diesels ('Whistlers'). I had photographed quite a few and now wanted a run behind one, so I spent a bit more time in the summer of 1964 on the LM main line trying to establish if they had any regular duties. This was regarded with some disdain by my fellow Southern enthusiasts as that summer was also the last of the ACE between Waterloo and Exeter and some fantastic performances were being turned in by the Merchant Navy Pacifics and their mainly Salisbury top link drivers, of which I was privileged to be present for quite a few. Word was that both the 11.25 am and 11.40 am from Euston on Saturdays were booked for Duchess haulage, but a visit on 1 August saw both Britannia-hauled, the 11.25 am with 70048 producing a dismal run to arrive at Rugby 17 minutes late. No luck there either though a fair number of steam hauled trains were to be seen. Timekeeping was abysmal that day and 70047 on the 11.40 am *Lakes* from Euston didn't pass Rugby until 1.59 pm! When 45672 arrived on the 339 pm up Blackpool, I gave up on seeing a Duchess and caught it back to Euston. Running very late it turned in a good solid performance, which was some consolation.

The next Saturday, 8 August, saw me back at Euston again, and this time my luck was in. A filthy 46228 *Duchess of Rutland* was standing at the head of the 11.25 am to Llandudno, first stop Rugby and 46245 *City of London* was on the 11.40 am Lakes Express, nominally non-stop to Wigan. Overjoyed I boarded the 13-coach 11.25 and we left on time to be banked up Camden bank. The schedule of 105 minutes wasn't very inspiring but I didn't care as at last I had my Duchess run. However we got no further than Kensal Green before being stopped briefly by signals. On the restart 46228 slipped violently but soon got the train going nicely, sailing quietly up to Tring before being stopped by signals before Cheddington; again quite briefly. We then ran the 47 miles to another signal stop outside Rugby in 48 minutes, with good spells of speed in the 70s interrupted by another signal check at Bletchley. I can only assume that we had been delayed on each occasion by the Class 40 hauled 11.15 am Euston to Holyhead, though we still managed to scrape into Rugby on time. We had only been standing 3 minutes when 46245 sailed through on the Lakes, having taken just 93 minutes from Euston and probably had been stopped behind us at Hillmorton. So I returned to London behind 70019 on the 3.39 pm up,

ORPINGTON TO ASHFORD

Date	Saturday 8 August 1964
Train	1125 am Euston to Llandudno
Loco	Class 8 4-6-2 No. 46228 *Duchess of Rutland*
Load	13 coaches, 432 tons tare, 465 tons gross
Weather	sunny periods
Recorder	Don Benn

	miles	sched	mins	secs	speed
Euston	0.00	0.00	00	00	
Camden No. 1	1.10		03	04	27/43
MP 5	5.00		sigs stop		0*
Willesden Junction	5.40		12	28	29
Wembley Central	8.05		16	47	43
Harrow	11.40		21	16	47½
Hatch End	13.30		23	46	50
Bushey	16.00		26	51	55
Watford Junction	17.45		28	22	61½
Kings Langley	20.95		31	57	58/60
Hemel Hempstead	24.50		35	44	56
Berkhamstead	27.95		39	40	53½
Tring	31.65		44	02	51
MP 35	35.00		sigs stop		0*
Cheddington	36.10		53	26	45
Sears Crossing	38.05		55	52	61
Leighton Buzzard	40.20		57	52	67
Stoke Hammond	44.00		61	02	74
Bletchley	46.65		64	48	29* sigs
Loughton	49.70		68	06	64½
Wolverton	52.40		70	25	72
Castlethorpe	54.75		72	25	70
Roade	59.90		77	08	64
Blisworth	62.85		79	50	70/77
Heyford	66.70		82	57	73
Weedon	69.70		85	24	72
Welton	75.30		90	09	67
Kilsby Tunnel North	78.40		92	46	73/75
Hillmorton	80.30		94	32	60* sigs
MP 82	82.00		sigs stop		0*
Rugby	82.55	105.00	104	20	
			net time 85 minutes		

well satisfied and now free to resume my Southern duties.

The sequel to this story is really quite amazing and shows once again what a small world us enthusiasts live in. Whilst trying to find photographs to accompany this little tale, a long time friend of mine, John Tiley, sent me a shot of 46228 restarting from a signal stop at Kensal Green. It turns out to have been the train I was on! I don't think I had met him by then, only doing so around a year later and so of course I had no idea he was there that day. If you look carefully you can see me looking out of the window in the first shot. Both images are courtesy of John Tiley, also a Southern man at heart.

No. 46225 *Duchess of Gloucester* passing Wembley on 24 August 1963 with the 8.40m am Carlisle to Euston.

Chapter Thirteen

1964 – The Last Year of the Atlantic Coast Express

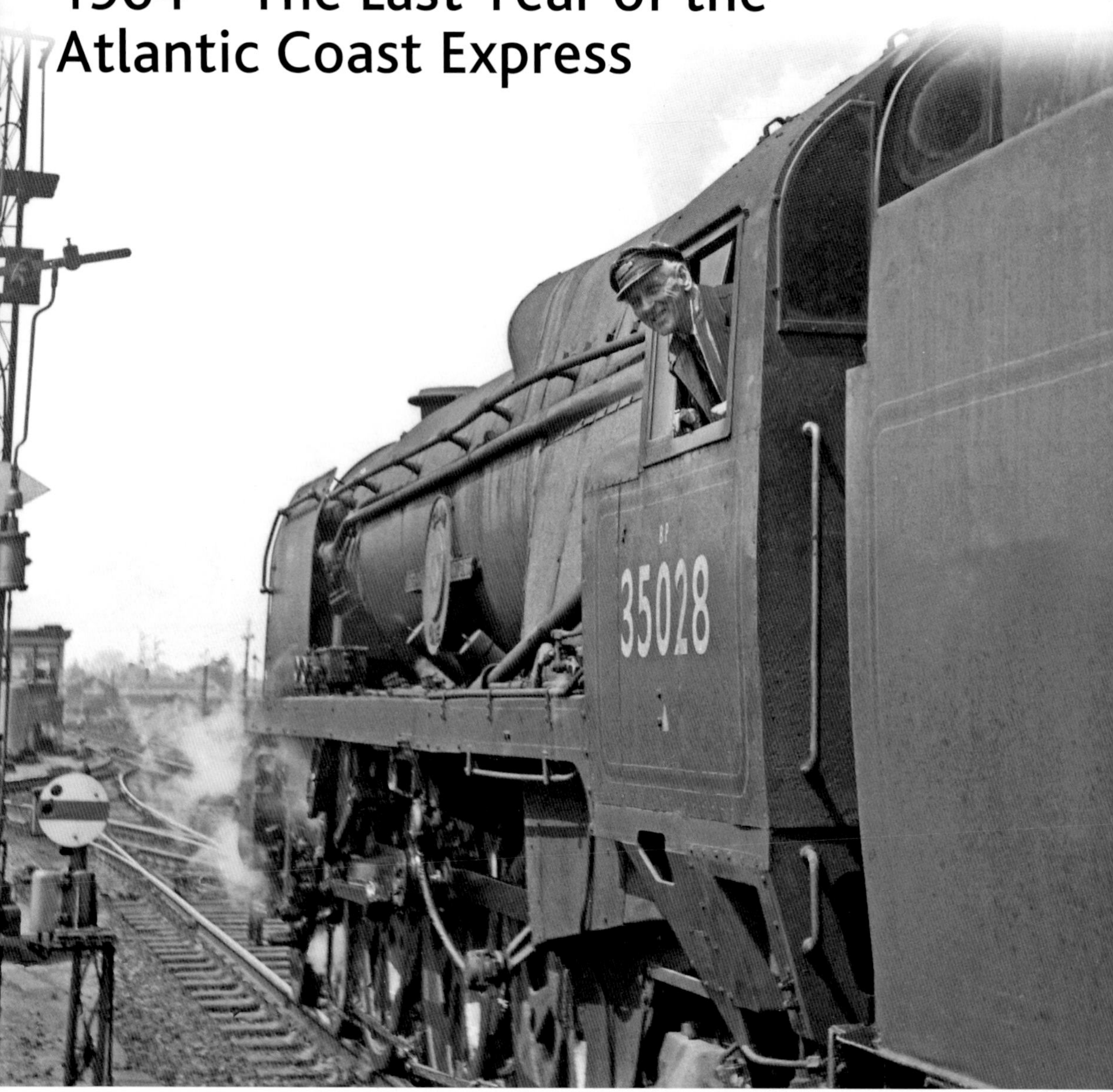

19 May 1964. Charlie Hopgood takes the 11 am from Waterloo out of Salisbury with 35028 *Clan Line*.

"These enginemen produced some very fine performances from their steeds, with good timekeeping a point of honour"

10 July 1963. 35009 *Shaw Savill* approaching Clapham Junction with the up ACE.

1964 was the last year of the famous Atlantic Coast Express (ACE) which ran from Waterloo to Exeter and beyond. This coincided with the transfer of the lines west of Salisbury from the Southern to the Western Region, the latter then doing its best to completely destroy the use made of the line by singling most of it and reducing the train service to a minimum. The ploy didn't work and now the line prospers and double track has been partly reinstated, most recently south of Chard Junction to Axminster.

In the 1960s for most of the year the ACE ran in one portion from Waterloo at 11 am, fast to Salisbury, then non-stop to Sidmouth Junction and Exeter Central. There the train would divide, with portions for Ilfracombe and Padstow. The up train, due at Waterloo at 3.29 pm, mirrored this arrangement and had the same timings over the two fastest sections. For three or four weeks at the height of the summer the train ran in two portions to and from Waterloo and Exeter, with the second down train at 11.05 am and the extra up train arriving at 3.21 pm. On summer Saturdays the train ran in five portions for all or part of the summer timetable, with Waterloo departures at 10.15, 10.35, 11.00, 11.15 and 11.45.

The accompanying table shows the motive power on these trains on 21 July 1962. This pattern continued right to the end of the summer timetable on 5 September in the last year of the ACE, 1964.

In the final three years the train was timed

WORTING JUNCTION - 21 JULY 1962

Train	Time	Engine	Load
1015 am Waterloo to Illfracombe and Torrington	1115 am	34054	11
1035 am Waterloo to Padstow and Bude	1130 am	73113	12
1045 am Waterloo to Seaton and Lyme Regis	1145 am	34010	12
1100 am Waterloo to Illfracombe and Torrington	1157 am	35018	13
1115 am Waterloo to Plymouth, Padstow and Bude	1212 pm	35014	12
1145 am Waterloo to Exmouth and Sidmouth	1245 pm	34068	12

23 July 1962. 35014 *Nederland Line* at Waterloo on the down ACE.

over the 83.7 miles to Salisbury in 80 minutes, and then 75 minutes (reduced to 73 minutes in 1964) for the 75.9 miles to Sidmouth Junction, making it the fastest booked steam hauled train on BR. With a load of 11 to 13 coaches it was booked for Merchant Navy haulage and for the last few years was worked both ways, between Waterloo and Salisbury by Salisbury men, and west of Salisbury by Exmouth Junction crews. These enginemen produced some very fine performances from their steeds, with good timekeeping a point of honour. I had many runs on the ACE, mostly between Waterloo and Salisbury and never had a bad run in the last two years. Time recovery from late running caused by delays earlier on the down runs could result in some quite fantastic performances from the Merchant Navy Pacifics. For instance on 30 May 1964 a signal failure at New Malden plus a late departure and a signal check at Tunnel Junction meant that 35012 on twelve coaches for 445 tons was 6 minutes late at Woking and 5 minutes late into Salisbury. Here Driver Cook and fireman Smith from Exmouth Junction took over and converted an 8 minute late departure into just 4 minutes late at Exeter. The time from Salisbury to Sidmouth Junction was just 71 minutes and 40 seconds with running of the highest quality throughout. The maximum speeds were 85 at Gillingham, 88 before Templecombe, 90 at Sherborne and 85 past Axminster. Honiton bank was climbed with a sustained minimum of 38mph, very good going with this load. The final dash from Sidmouth Junction produced another 90 through the woods at Broad Clyst. Even better was on 29 February 1964 when driver Besley of Exmouth Junction left Salisbury no less than 12 minutes late with 35020 on eleven coaches for 400 tons and reached Exeter just 2 minutes late.

The time from Salisbury to Sidmouth Junction was 69 minutes 38 seconds with some very fast speeds on the downhill sections: 91 at Gillingham, 83 before Templecombe, no less than 96 at Sherborne and 91 at Axminster. Honiton was climbed at a minimum of 41mph, my highest on the ACE. The overall time for the 88 miles from Salisbury to Exeter was a very fine 85 minutes 44 seconds. That was my fastest and included over 2½ minutes standing at Sidmouth Junction.

Before I look at more runs in that last year of 1964 I must mention the Salisbury drivers who covered the train both ways between Waterloo and Salisbury (except on Bank Holidays). During the period 1961 to 1963 the Salisbury top link drivers were:- Doc Allen, Tom Hatcher, Bill

11 April 1964, 35024 *East Asiatic Company* passing Surbiton on the down ACE.

Brownscombe, Ernie Pistell, Bert Cambray (always smartly dressed with a bow tie), Dick Hurrell, Walter Clissold, Ted Britten, Fred Hoare, Ed Saunders, Sid Bowden and Percy Young. As some of these retired they were replaced by others from lower links or the spare link and these men also covered for absence from time to time. They included Simms, Phillips, Cox, Tutt, Knight, Sharpe, Hill, Padwick, Hooper, Charlie Hopgood and Sid Burton. I got to know many of the regular drivers quite well, particularly the Salisbury men, most in their last years before retirement. All of these drivers were capable of timing the ACE easily with a Merchant Navy and some could if a Bulleid light Pacific was allocated, which sometimes happened especially on the up train. Others though would take the view that a light Pacific couldn't do the job and so set out with that in mind and drove the engine as if it were a Merchant which usually resulted in a loss of about three minutes on the schedule between Salisbury and Waterloo. Men like Fred Hoare though relished the prospect of the smaller engine and kept time easily.

Fred had a particular liking for the unrebuilt engines and reckoned they were freer running than the Jarvis rebuilds, which I agree with and have stated elsewhere. The 80 minute schedule, especially going down, could be kept very easily provided that a good start was made and the climbs to milepost 31, Battledown and Grateley were taken well. Speed barely needed to reach 80 for a timekeeping run and indeed my fastest down run in 76 minutes 4 seconds was done with a maximum speed of 82mph. Although the up train was generally regarded as being the tougher proposition, both Doc Allen and Ed Saunders gave me runs of just under 80

3 June 1963. 35020 *Bibby Line* near Pirbright with the down ACE.

12 October 1963. 35019 *French Line* CGT on the down ACE passing Walton-on-Thames.

WATERLOO TO SALISBURY

Date	6 June 1964					18 April 1964		
Train	11 am Waterloo-Salisbury					11 am Waterloo-Salisbury		
Loco	MN class 4-6-2 No. 35026 *Lamport and Holt Line*					MN class 4-6-2 No. 35016 *Elders Fyffes*		
Load	12 cars 409½ tons tare, 445 tons gross					12 coaches, 407 tons tare, 435 tons gross		
Driver	C Hopgood, Salisbury					Cox, Salisbury. Inspector Jupp		
Fireman	unknown					unknown		
Weather	fine and warm					fine and warm		
	miles	sched	mins	secs	speed	mins	secs	speed
Waterloo	0.00	0.00	00	00		00	00	
Vauxhall	1.29		03	23	36/47½	03	37	37/54½
Clapham Junction	3.93	7.00	07	01	41*	06	53	43*
Wimbledon	7.24		11	17	57	10	48	56
New Malden	9.78		13	45	64½	13	19	63½
Surbiton	12.04		15	44	70½	15	21	70
Hampton Court Jct	13.34	17.30	16	48	75	16	26	71
Esher	14.39		17	40	77	17	19	74
Hersham	15.91		18	54	76	18	35	75
Walton	17.08		19	48	75/72	19	32	72½/71
Weybridge	19.15		21	30	74	21	14	73
Byfleet	20.40		22	33	77	22	16	77½
West Byfleet	21.68		23	36	73/64* sigs	23	17	74
Woking	24.29		25	55	67	25	30	71½
Woking Jct	24.75	27.00	26	18	68	25	50	70
Brookwood	27.99		29	14	68½	28	42	67½
MP 31	31.00		32	00	64½	31	31	62½
Farnborough	33.20		34	00	71	33	28	71½
Fleet	36.48		36	43	75/78	36	07	77/79
Winchfield	39.83		39	21	76/73	38	41	76½/75
Hook	42.16		41	18	74/72	40	34	78/75½
Newnham Siding	43.70		42	33	76	41	42	81
Basingstoke	47.75		45	55	71	44	57	66*
Worting Jct	50.30	50.00	48	08	65	47	06	65½
Oakley	52.38		50	04	70	49	06	70
Overton	55.55		52	44	77	51	42	78
Whitchurch	59.10		55	26	82	54	30	79
Hurstbourne	61.14		56	51	84/79	56	52	pws 24*
Andover	66.35		60	43	85	62	27	76½
Red Post Jct	67.65		61	47	78½/80	63	36	74/75
Grateley	72.70		65	51	66	67	53	60
Allington Box	75.60		68	21	75	70	24	69½
Porton	78.29		70	21	82/86½	72	43	78/84
Tunnel Junction	82.56		74	24	sigs 25*/48	78	05	sigs 16*/43
Salisbury	83.66	80.00	76	58		81	02	
	net time 76 mins Waterloo depart R/T					net time 76 mins Waterloo depart R/T		

minutes unchecked with a maximum speed of 80mph. True enginemanship with trains running on time.

I have picked out two 1964 runs each way over the Waterloo to Salisbury section as this is where I did most of my travelling. Both were very fine runs with drivers who came later to the Salisbury top link and both had the normal 'winter' load of twelve coaches 435-445 tons full. Both also had exactly the same net time of 76 minutes and were fairly typical of down runs in that last year, showing just how much time a Merchant Navy with a good driver had to spare on the 80 minute schedule. Charlie Hopgood was a very consistent driver and a cheerful character as can be seen from one of the photographs. I had a series of similar runs with him at the regulator. The 85mph overall speed limit wasn't often exceeded on this stretch even when making up lost time, though it was a different matter after Salisbury, as referred to earlier in the article. Driver Cox would have got us into Salisbury more than minute early on 18 April if it

SALISBURY TO WATERLOO

Date	18 April 1964					24 April 1964		
Train	209 pm Salisbury-Waterloo					209 pm Salisbury-Waterloo		
Engine	MN Class 4-6-2 No. 35013 *Blue Funnel*					MN Class 4-6-2 No. 35025 *Lamport and Holt Line*		
Load	11 cars 372 tons tare, 400 tons gross					11 cars 372 tons tare, 400 tons gross		
Driver	Tutt, Salisbury					Sid Burton, Salisbury		
Fireman	Young, Salisbury					Unknown		
Weather	fine and warm					fine and warm		
	miles	sched	mins	secs	speed	mins	secs	speed
Salisbury	0.00	0.00	00	00		00	00	
Tunnel Junction	1.10		03	27	37	03	12	37
Porton	5.37		09	31	45½/41	08	46	51½/49
Allington Box	8.06		13	05	50	11	54	56
Grateley	10.96		16	17	61½/77	14	42	67/83
Red Post Jct	16.01		20	29	74½	17	46	79
Andover	17.31		21	35	79	19	42	83
MP 62½	21.16		24	49	66	22	52	64
Hurstbourne	22.52		26	37	pws 23*	24	09	71
Whitchurch	24.56		30	13	45	26	00	67
Overton	28.11		34	25	60	29	06	72½
Oakley	31.28		37	26	67½	31	41	77
Worting Jct	33.36	34.00	39	18	70	33	20	78
Basingstoke	35.91		41	17	80/86½	35	16	79
Hook	41.50		45	17	81/82½	39	38	73
Winchfield	43.83		47	03	81/85	41	31	78/82
Fleet	47.18		49	28	83	44	01	80½
Farnborough	50.46		51	51	80	46	30	80
MP 31	52.66		53	34	78	48	16	76½
Brookwood	55.67		55	46	84	50	30	84/88
Woking Jct	58.91	54.00	58	10	76*	52	43	85
Woking	59.37		58	29	79	53	07	86
West Byfleet	61.98		60	27	83	55	01	83
Byfleet	63.26		61	22	86	55	56	84
Weybridge	64.51		62	17	83/80	56	54	79/75½
Walton	66.58		63	47	82½	58	30	79
Hersham	67.75		64	38	83	59	22	80
Esher	69.27		65	46	80	60	32	80½
Hampton Court Jct	70.32	63.30	66	34	81	61	23	80
Surbiton	71.62		67	33	80/77½	62	27	73/70½
New Malden	73.88		69	17	79	64	20	73
Wimbledon	76.42		71	19	74	66	40	65
Clapham Junction	79.73	73.00	74	44	*44/56½	70	06	*45/55
Vauxhall	82.37		78	01	43*	73	28	44*
Waterloo	83.66	80.00	81	07		76	50	
	net time 76½ minutes depart Salisbury 2 mins late arrive Waterloo 3 mins late Basingstoke to Wimbledon 81.0mph					depart Salisbury 7 mins late arrive Waterloo 4 mins late Basingstoke to Wimbledon 77.4mph		

hadn't been for the signal check at Tunnel Junction, despite the relaying slack at Hurstbourne. Another of the photographs shows 35016 after arrival at Salisbury.

The two up runs tabulated are also typical of what was being done that year, or maybe above par for the course as anything under 78 minutes was considered to be good. On 18 April, having gone down on the ACE we decided to return on the up train and were rewarded with a very good run with one of the spare link drivers, Tutt. The start was quite steady with the engine priming on the climb up Porton bank and it wasn't until after the relaying slack at Hurstbourne that *Blue Funnel* really got going averaging exactly 81mph from Basingstoke to Wimbledon, without exceeding 86mph and with an easing to 76mph through Woking. This was one of my fastest times over the 25.55 mile section from Worting Junction to Woking Junction

13 July 1963. Just west of Woking. The down ACE headed by 35001 passing the 11.25 Woking to Salisbury local headed by 31631.

18 April 1964. 35016 *Elders Fyffes* at Salisbury after the run described above.

8 June 1963. 35030 *Elder Dempster Lines* heads the down ACE at Raynes Park.

as on many runs the running was only just enough to keep the very tight 20 minute booking which required an average speed of nearly 77mph and a clear road.

If you add the time from Salisbury to Worting Junction of the run on 24 April to the time of this run in from there you get an overall time of 75 minutes 9 seconds which wasn't often achieved in practice. In fact the time of 41 minutes 49 seconds for the 50.30 miles in from Worting Junction was the fastest I ever recorded with steam. 35013 *Blue Funnel* worked the up ACE a lot in 1964 and I had more runs with this consistently good engine than any other. The 24 April run was timed as part of a week's Southern Rail Rover and Sid Burton worked the up ACE most of the week. He was a lovely man and a good driver though went better with a bit of encouragement. This was his best run of the week with a very good start and some faster than normal running down past Woking. I suspect he had an eye on the clock and thought he might be able to recover all of the seven minute late start. He didn't but it was my fastest time of the week and indeed my fastest ever on the up ACE. Sid Burton gave me two other runs on the up ACE that week. On 22 April he had 35013 with the usual eleven coaches for 400 tons. The overall time was 81 minutes 53 seconds with a signal check from the up Salisbury stopper at West Byfleet which we caught again at Wimbledon. Net time was just over 77 minutes, showing consistency with the run on 24 April, and on 23 April Sid had unrebuilt light pacific 34086 on the same load.

We had an unchecked run in 81 minutes 37 seconds, being slower out to Worting but running in from there in 44 minutes 41 seconds, over a minute better than the schedule.

It all came to an end when 35022 worked the last down Atlantic Coast Express on 4 September 1964 and with it the last express train running to mile-a-minute timings. Though I timed many very good runs after that year and before the end of steam on the Southern, the ACE remains the high water mark with so many good runs and memories of those true enginemen, especially the Salisbury men.

9 March 1962. 35025 *Brocklebank Line* on the up ACE passing Vauxhall.

17 July 1962. Driver Percy Young of Salisbury on 35018 *British India Line* at Waterloo about to depart on the ACE.

Chapter Fourteen

Scotland – Autumn 1964

31 October 1964. 60009 *Union of South Africa* leaving Stirling with the 7.10 am Aberdeen to Glasgow.

"The engine was spotless and our driver as far as Perth, John Thompson, gave us a characteristically solid performance"

1 November 1964. 46160 *Queen Victoria's Rifleman* on shed at Polmadie.

This was my first full trip to Scotland. I accompanied a friend from my Southern steam exploits, the very knowledgeable John Evans, who unfortunately is no longer around. Without John this unadventurous 19-year-old would not have ventured forth in such style as John not only knew the area, including the hotels, but had also secured shed passes for our Sunday shed bash. So it was that I found myself on the 7.30 pm Kings Cross to Aberdeen behind Deltic No D9010, the first of many journeys on this train. From Edinburgh we were hauled to our destination by EE type 4 No D326, reached three minutes early and in time for breakfast in the buffet. Then we joined the 7.10 am three hour train to Glasgow, six coaches hauled by one of Gresley's splendid A4 pacifics, No 60009 *Union of South Africa*, which is fortunately preserved and still on the main line today. The engine was spotless and our driver as far as Perth, John Thompson, gave us a characteristically solid performance, keeping the schedule to the first stop at Stonehaven and then running the 41.65 miles to Forfar at an average speed of 60.4mph, with a maximum speed of 80mph at Laurencekirk.

30 October 1964, Stirling. 45168 on the 9.40 am Callander to Edinburgh.

TABLE ONE – FORFAR TO PERTH

Date	Friday 30 October 1964
Train	710 am Aberdeen to Glasgow
Loco	A4 Class 4-6-2 No 60009 *Union of South Africa*
Load	6 coaches, 208 tons tare, 225 tons gross
Driver	John Thompson, Ferryhll
Weather	Calm and Cloudy
Position	2 of 6

	miles	sched	mins	secs	speed
Forfar	0.00	0.00	00	00	
Forfar South Box	0.70		02	10	40
Kirriemuir Box	2.85		04	32	67½
Glamis	5.65		06	55	75
Eassie	7.85		08	35	80/82½
Alyth Junction	11.90	12.00	11	37	79/82
Ardler Box	13.15		12	30	77½
Ardler	14.20		13	25	75
Coupar Angus	16.65		15	20	78/81
Burrelton	18.85		17	07	75
Cargill	21.20		18	56	84
Ballathie	23.05		20	21	75/77
Stanley Junction	25.30	23.00	22	13	74
Strathord	27.35		23	46	79½
Luncarty	28.30		24	37	77
Almond Valley Jct	30.85		26	44	72½
Perth	32.50	32.00	29	38	
	start to stop average 65.8mph				

TABLE TWO – GLENEAGLES TO PERTH

Date	Friday 30 October 1964
Train	925 am Crewe to Perth
Loco	Rebuilt Scot 4-6-0 No 46160 *Queen Victoria's Rifleman*
Load	5 coaches and 3 vans, 254 tons tare, 275 tons gross
Weather	calm and cloudy
Position	2 of 6

	miles	sched	mins	secs	speed
Gleneagles	0.00	0.00	00	00	
MP 237	1.55		02	32	57
Auchterarder	2.05		03	04	60
MP 140	4.55		05	23	67
Dunning	6.20		06	52	72
Forteviot	8.95		09	32	62/70
Forgandenny	11.85		12	04	67½/70
Hilton Junction	13.75		13	43	66
Friarton	14.84		15	13	*52
Perth	15.75	20.00	17	32	

On to Perth we did even better over this racing stretch, covering the 32.5 miles at a start to stop average of 65.8mph, thus gaining time on the schedule and arriving over two minutes early. The log of this section is shown in Table One. The maximum of 84mph over the river at Cargill wasn't unusual on this train, despite the 75mph limit applying throughout Scotland. A fresh crew took us on to Stirling nicely inside schedule and here we alighted in order to return to Stonehaven on the 10.47 am train behind Type 4 No D337, to catch the 1.30 pm semi-fast train from Aberdeen, also booked for A4 haulage. There was still a profusion of steam in the area, many being Stanier Black 5s; in total that day I noted no less than thirty-one different engines in steam or working trains, including No 55204, a McIntosh 0-4-4 tank built in 1910 and withdrawn just after our visit.

Our A4 on the 1.30 pm from Aberdeen was No 60016 *Silver King* with a load of seven plus a van, totalling around 300 tons and this performed well, without any fireworks, to deposit us at Gleneagles four minutes early. We had just failed to achieve even time from Forfar to Coupar Angus despite a maximum speed of 77mph. There we picked up the 9.25 am Crewe to Perth semi-fast train, which we were to catch from Carlisle the next day; a train which was capable of producing almost anything as motive power. Today we had rebuilt Scot No 46160 *Queen Victoria's Rifleman* on five coaches and three vans and this ran with very little effort down the hill to Perth, arriving on time. The log is shown in Table Two. Here we booked in to the North British Hotel next to the station before returning for some more steam mileage, this time on the line to Dundee.

First we caught a DMU on the 5.33 pm out to Invergowrie, returning with BR Standard Class 5 No 73150 on six coaches, then another BR Standard Caprotti Class 5 No 73152 on eight for about 285 tons which did well to keep the tight 15 minute booking to Errol providing lots of noise in the process (Table Three). Finally we returned to Perth behind Stanier Class 5 No 44718 for a meal and an early night. This engine was in immaculate ex works condition and ran into Perth three minutes early.

The next day, a Saturday, our objective was Carlisle and the aforementioned 9.25 am Crewe to Perth train which we had caught from Gleneagles the previous

1 November 1964. B1 61099 with A4 60010 on shed at St Margarets.

day. Our southbound train was to be the diesel hauled 9 am Perth to London Euston, but first we caught the 8.51 am from Perth to Stirling, which was the 7.10 am from Aberdeen, again hauled by *Union of South Africa* and again with the same 6-coach load. This produced a good run up the climb to Gleneagles with speed sustained at 47mph over the last mile of 1 in 101, before a carefree dash down to Dunblane with scant regard to the 75 mph limit, as shown in Table Four.

At Stirling we picked up the 9 am from Perth hauled by EE Type 4 No D303 on nine coaches and this had little problem keeping the easy schedule with only marginal excesses above 75mph. The log is shown in Table Five. At Carlisle it soon became apparent that the engine for our train back to Scotland would be a BR Class 6 'Clan' and so No 72006 *Clan Mackenzie* gave me my one and only run behind one of these unloved (and unwanted?) machines. With just five coaches and a van for 220 tons it was well up to the task with no great effort required (Table Six). We left the train

TABLE THREE – PERTH TO ERROL

Date	Friday 30th October 1964
Train	615 pm Glasgow Buchanan Street to Dundee
Loco	BR Standard Caprotti Class 5 4-6-0 No. 73152
Load	8 coaches, 268 tons tare, 285 tons gross
Weather	calm and cloudy
Position	front

	miles	sched	mins	secs	speed
Perth	0.00	0.00	00	00	
Princes Street	0.40		02	10	41
Kinfauns	3.55		06	52	64½/65½
Glencarse	6.30		09	33	64/56½
Inchcoonans Box	9.10		12	28	60
Errol	10.25	15.00	14	51	

TABLE FOUR – PERTH TO STIRLING

Date	Saturday 31 October 1964
Train	710 am Aberdeen to Glasgow
Loco	A4 Class 4-6-2 No 60009 *Union of South Africa*
Load	6 coaches, 208 tons tare, 225 tons gross
Weather	dry, cold

	miles	sched	mins	secs	speed
Perth	0.00	0.00	00	00	
Hilton Junction	2.10	4.00	04	40	50
Forgandenny	4.00		06	37	64/66
Forteviot	6.90		09	18	65/66½
Dunning	9.65		11	59	64
MP 141	10.30		12	41	60
MP 140	11.30		13	46	54½
MP 139	12.30		14	53	53
MP 138	13.30		16	06	49½
Auchterarder	13.80		16	35	49
MP 137	14.30		17	21	48½
MP 136	15.30		18	37	47½
Gleneagles	15.85	19.00	19	00	47
MP 135	16.30		19	52	47
Blackford	18.05		21	39	65½
Carsebreck Box	20.30		23	54	79/78
Greenloaning	22.30		25	08	80/82
Kinbuck	25.50		27	38	*72/79
Dunblane	28.15	31.00	29	50	*64/70½
Bridge of Allen	30.20		31	41	*67/73
Cornton Box	31.15		32	36	72
Stirling	33.05	36.00	34	56	

TABLE FIVE – CARSTAIRS TO CARLISLE

Date	Saturday 31 October 1964
Train	9 am Perth to Euston
Loco	EE Type 4 1Co-Co1 No. D303
Load	9 coaches, 304 tons tare, 330 tons gross
Weather	dry, cold

	miles	sched	mins	secs	speed
Carstairs	0.00	0.00	00	00	on time
Leggafoot Box	3.60		05	35	53½
Thankerton	5.05		07	07	66
Symington	6.70		08	44	58
Lamington	10.40		12	30	71½/tsr *44
Abington	15.80		18	07	61½
Crawford	18.35		20	34	64/60
Elvanfoot	20.80		23	07	66½
Beattock Summit	23.90		26	00	51
Harthope	25.80		27	54	72/*66
Greskine	28.20		29	53	76 max
Beattock	33.90	40.00	36	06	
	0.00	0.00	00	00	
Murthat	2.70		03	55	67/75
Wamphray	5.20		06	10	72½/65½
Dinwoodie	8.00		08	34	72½
Nethercleugh	11.05		11	01	76
Lockerbie	13.95	15.00	14	21	
	0.00	0.00	00	00	
Castlemilk Siding	3.05		06	09	54½
Ecclefechan	5.60		07	28	75
Kirtlebridge	9.05		10	55	tsr *33
Kirkpatrick	12.80		15	11	75
Gretna Junction	17.05		18	42	77
Floriston	19.60		20	50	68½
Rockcliffe	21.60		22	32	71
Kingmoor	23.65		24	16	70
Carlisle	25.65	31.00	26	51	
					5 mins early

at Larbert where arrival was nearly four minutes early and caught a DMU to Glasgow before booking into the Caledonian Hotel, just down from Buchanan Street station. The plan then was to catch the 5.30 pm to Perth behind another A4 Pacific but although my companion did this I decided to catch up on some lost sleep and so stayed behind. That day I recorded another thirty-five engines in steam or working trains, again mainly Stanier Class 5s. 76070, 42129 and 42214 were noted at Beattock waiting to bank northbound trains up the hill.

We were up bright and early the next day, a Sunday, as this was shed bash day. It started by catching a number 7a bus to Polmadie where thirty-five engines were on shed including No 46160 from our run on Friday, and two Class A2 Pacifics, 60524 and 60527, both then still in service. By bus back to Glasgow and then the 10.45 am from Queen Street to Falkirk Grahamston and another bus to Grangemouth shed. Here there were twenty-seven engines, many dumped including J37 0-6-0 freight locos Nos. 64580 and 64636. Grangemouth shed would close a year later. Then it was bus back to Falkirk for the 1.34 pm train to Edinburgh Haymarket and another bus to St Margarets shed, changing in Princes Street and alighting at Clockmill Road.

At St Margarets we had our only slightly hostile reception though we were allowed round. Here were quite a few express passenger engines in the form of Gresley's A3 and A4 Pacifics plus an A1 and a number of V2s.

In total there were forty on shed mostly in steam, the biggest surprise being the large number of B1 4-6-0s, one of which, 61244, would work to Hawick the next day. It was just a pity that the drab weather which had been with us so far continued through the day and so it was beginning to get dark as we caught the number 4 bus to Waverley to get a meal.

31 October 1964. 72006 *Clan Mackenzie* stands at Carlisle waiting to take the 9.25 am Crewe to Perth forward.

TABLE SIX – CARLISLE TO CARSTAIRS

Date	Saturday 31 October 1964
Train	925 am Crewe to Perth
Loco	Class 6 4-6-2 No 72006 *Clan Mackenzie*
Load	5 coaches and 1 van, 202 tons tare, 220 tons gross
Weather	dry, cold

	miles	sched	mins	secs	speed
Carlisle	0.00	0.00	00	00	
Kingmoor	2.08		03	44	48½
Rockcliffe	4.08		06	00	62
Floriston	6.09		07	54	66½/72
Gretna Junction	8.72		10	08	66
Quintinshill	10.16		11	46	56½
Kirkpatrick	13.01		15	06	50
Kirtlebridge	16.72		19	52	trs 37*
Ecclefechan	20.10		24	24	49/56½
Castlemilk Siding	22.60		27	35	sigs 49*/45*
Lockerbie	25.84		31	15	58
Dinwoodie	31.77		37	10	64/66½
Wamphray	34.50		40	01	60
Murthat	36.90		42	58	sigs 47*
Beattock	39.76		46	24	51
MP 41	41.00		48	06	43
MP 42	42.00		49	36	38½
MP 43	43.00		51	18	35
MP 44	44.00		53	07	33
MP 45	45.00		55	01	31
Greskine	45.35		55	46	31
MP 46	46.00		56	57	33
MP 47	47.00		58	44	35
Harthope	47.70		59	52	34
MP 48	48.00		60	27	33½
MP 49	49.00		62	18	32
Beattock Summit	49.76		63	41	31
Elvanfoot	52.65		67	04	65/70
Crawford	55.14		69	31	67/64
Abington	57.90		71	50	67½/62
Wandlemill	60.31		74	20	70½/66½
Lamington	63.23		76	50	73
Symington	66.70		80	07	64
Thankerton	68.50		81	39	72/75
Leggafoot Box	70.10		82	54	72
Carstairs	73.65	88.00	86	56	
	net time 83½ minutes edbh MP 47 to Beattock Summit = 1,020				

Then came the final shed visit of the day, which was to Dunfermline, gained by catching the 5.20 pm DMU from Waverley to Dunfermline Lower and then walking. Here in the pitch black we found the foreman asleep and so wandered round quietly bagging a total of eighteen, mostly in steam, including five WD 2-10-0s and two 1888 built Holmes J36 0-6-0s. After this clandestine visit John and I decided to part company as he wanted to cover the B1 turn in from Hawick the next day and I wanted another run on the 7.10 am from Aberdeen. So I caught the 7.03 pm from Dunfermline Lower to Waverley and then the 8 pm to Glasgow before boarding the 11.10 pm from Glasgow Queen Street to Aberdeen which was hauled by D5126 to Perth and A4 No 60006 *Sir Ralph Wedgwood* from there. Surprisingly I remember nothing of this journey or of what must have been a long and cold wait at Aberdeen after arrival at 3.05 am on Monday morning until gaining the warmth of the 7.10 am three-hour train. This was once again hauled by A4 No 60009 *Union of South Africa* on six coaches, turning in another faultless performance with another even time run from Stonehaven to Forfar and a time of 29 minutes 31 seconds on to Perth, an average of 66.1mph with a maximum speed of 83 over the river at Cargill.

By now I had run out of both film and money so decided to wait at Perth for the next steam hauled train to Glasgow, which was the 10 am from Dundee to Glasgow semi-fast two-hour train on very tight timings. It duly appeared running late and to my delight had Jubilee 5XP 4-6-0 No 45742 *Connaught*, last of the class, on nine well filled coaches for about 330 tons. It was so busy I had to stand but well worth it for the sparkling performance turned in by the Jub and her footplate crew. We were 19 minutes late away and I was treated to some superb Jubilee three cylinder roar as we stormed out of Perth and up the climb to Gleneagles. As speed dropped on the 1 in 100 so the noise increased and speed stabilised at 44mph over the last mile of the climb, which according to my calculations meant that the Jub was putting out 1,500 equivalent drawbar horsepower, a very high figure for a Class 6 engine, and my highest with a Jubilee, not even being surpassed by the efforts of *Leander* or *Kolhapur* in their later years on the main line. In fact the big effort continued throughout to Glasgow, reached 15 minutes late unchecked but with over time at all station stops due to

Polmadie 1/11/64

42143
42176
45120
80115
45588
80109
80058
73055
46160
73062
60535
80106
80118
80107
80108
73099
80116
42274
73059
80120
80001
73098
42277
80002.
73061
46160 (P7&8)

42241
44791
73060
73005
60522
44986
80130
60527
60524
42243
(37)

Cravgenroult

90600
77009
73007
90560
76113.
44788
77006
44970
76102
76103
44719.

45362
90489.
64592.
46468.
76101
64621.
76045.
90199
45319.
45177
45443.
45192.
76046.
64580 (P9)
64636
90553

St Margarets

60813
61294
45461
60010
61099 (P10)
76064
60100 (P11)
60024 (P12)
44903
80055
61275
46462
61345
60846
60835
80003
65929
60152
61397
60052
61354
61404
44669
61245
61344
61244
60836

80022.
61349
80122
42691.
80114
80026
80006
80007
65914
65915
80112
69128
65234.

Dunfermline

65327
65918
76109
61072
64555
64599
90547
64623
90229
64611
90071

90515
90534
65288.
65931
90039
65921
61101

61244 Edinburgh 2/11/64
4.00 Galashiels.
4.10 Hawick

73/45 spd
ex 7.15 Dundee.

Perth 2/11/64

60970
44925
44959
42128 Dunblane.
45389
76046

St Margarets 2/11/64

61191
80022

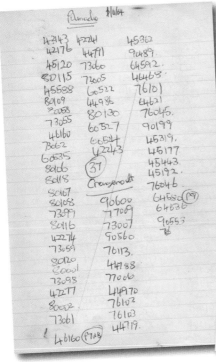

1 November 1964, Polmadie shed. 46160 *Queen Victoria's Rifleman* with a couple of BR class 4 tanks and 73061.

1 November 1964, St Margarets Shed. 60100 *Spearmint.*

1 November 1964, St Margarets shed. 60010 *Dominion of Canada* with 60100 *Spearmint*, 61294 and 61099.

1 November 1964, Grangemouth shed.
J37 No 64580.

the heavy volume of passengers. Details of the run as far as Stirling are shown in Table Seven. For me this run was the highlight of the trip and well worth the night of lost sleep. From Buchanan Street I crossed Glasgow to Queen Street and caught the 1.30 pm DMU to Waverley where, reunited with my friend we boarded the 4 pm to Kings Cross *Talisman*, seven coaches and four Pullmans headed by Deltic D9020 *Nimbus*. We enjoyed a steak meal as the Deltic whisked us south to arrive in Kings Cross just a few minutes late after some very fast running up to 105mph, and with an extra stop at Darlington and delays in the Hitchin area. So ended the first of many forays north of the border, mainly to time the Gresley Pacifics in their last days.

TABLE SEVEN – PERTH TO STIRLING

Date	Monday 2 November 1964
Train	10 am Dundee West to Glasgow
Loco	5XP Jubilee Class 4-6-0 No 45742 *Connaught*
Load	9 coaches, 306 tons tare, 330 tons gross
Weather	dry and bright

	miles	sched	mins	secs	speed
Perth	0.00	0.00	00	00	19¼ mins late
Hilton Junction	2.10	4.00	04	56	43
Forgandenny	4.00		07	12	54½
Forteviot	6.90		10	04	64/60½
Dunning	9.65		12	47	62
MP 141	10.30		13	35	57
MP 140	11.30		14	42	53
MP 139	12.30		15	53	51
MP 138	13.30		17	10	47½
Auchterarder	13.80		17	39	46
MP 137	14.30		18	30	44
MP 136	15.30		19	51	44
Gleneagles	15.85	21.00	20	41	
	0.00	0.00	00	00	slipping
MP 134½	0.95		03	06	38
Blackford	2.20		04	33	55½
Carsebreck Box	4.45		06	45	67/65
Greenloaning	6.45		08	37	67½/72
Kinbuck	9.65		11	25	67½/70
Dunblane	12.30	15.00	14	17	
	0.00	0.00	00	00	
Bridge of Allen	2.05		03	02	65½
Cornton Box	3.00		04	01	70
Stirling	4.90	7.00	06	16	18 mins late
					1500 edbh MPs 137-136

Chapter Fifteen

4.49 pm East Croydon to London Bridge

8 July 1963 Redhill.
4 LAV 2949 passing
U class 31791.

"I soon realised that the 4.49 up was a very rare and interesting train"

449 pm EAST CROYDON TO LONDON BRIDGE – SCHEDULE 15 MINS													
Run No.	1					2				3			
Date	6 January 1967					2 February 1967				3 February 1967			
Units	4SUB 4289 +2 x 4 LAVS=12					4LAV 2953 + 2 x 4LAVS=12 LAV				4LAV 2923 + 2 x 4LAV=12 LAV			
Driver	James, Reigate					James, Reigate				James, Reigate			
	miles	time	mins	secs	speed	time	mins	secs	speed	time	mins	secs	speed
East Croydon	0.00	1½ L	00	00		5 L	00	00		16 L	00	00	
Windmill Bridge Jct	0.50		00	59	42		00	55	40		00	59	41½
Norwood Junction	1.67		02	24	54		02	37	53½		02	26	54
MP 8¼	2.11		02	59	55½		03	08	54½		02	58	55½
Anerley	2.77		03	36	58		03	51	56		03	38	57
Penge West	3.17		04	04	60		04	18	59		04	06	59
Sydenham	3.86		04	47	64		05	02	60½		04	49	62½
Forest Hill	4.73		05	34	65½		05	47	63		05	37	64
MP 5½	4.86		05	43	66½		05	56	64½		05	45	65½
Honor Oak Park	5.62		06	21	70		06	36	72		06	25	70
MP 4	6.36		06	57	75		07	11	76		07	02	75
Brockley	6.66		07	10	78		07	25	80		07	16	78
MP 3½	6.86		07	20	80		07	33	82		07	25	80
New Cross Gate	7.48		07	48	*66		07	58	*70		07	52	*72
Bricklayers Arms Jct	8.71		08	38	*50		08	46	*63/60		08	43	*51 sigs
Spa Road	9.21		09	57	55½/sigs 26*		09	47	61½		10	15	52/sigs 16*
London Bridge	10.36	1½ E	12	14		1½ L	11	43		14 L	12	54	
	net time 12 mins					net time 11¾ mins				net time 11¾ mins			
	* brakes/speed restriction												

During 1966 I worked in the Materials and Progressing Section at Southern Region HQ at Waterloo, my job entailing moving the stocks of spares for the remaining steam engines around between depots to keep the engines working. The spares stocks for modern traction had been centralised under the CM&EE and therefore my application for promotion to the Accounts section of the CM&EE at Southern House, Croydon in December 1966 was a natural career progression. At that time I was still living at home in Shirley, near West Wickham but rarely did I go straight home after work. As steam still clung on out of Waterloo until July 1967 and I was engaged to be married to a young lady who also worked on the railway and lived at Tunbridge Wells, my normal journey after work ended at 4.30 pm each day, at least until the end of steam. I would catch the 4.49 pm East Croydon to London Bridge, whence I could either catch one of the remaining steam hauled trains out of Waterloo, or meet the aforesaid young lady or a combination of both!

I soon realised that the 4.49 up was a very rare and interesting train, for it was a 12 LAV formation originating from Reigate and after arrival at London Bridge forming one of the last main line workings with LAVs, probably returning on the 17.26 to Reigate. Whilst my main interest was timing steam hauled trains I had always timed a selection of modern traction and retain the same balanced view on matters to this day.

In theory a 60mph speed limit applied in the suburban area out as far as South Croydon but scant regard was paid to this in those far off pre spy-in-the-cab and HSE days. The line from East Croydon to London Bridge starts with the continuation of the 1 in 264 fall from the North Downs and then levels out before Norwood Junction after which it is level or slightly downhill to the north end of Forest Hill station where the line then falls steeply at 1 in 100 until just before New Cross Gate station, a distance of 2.70

449 pm EAST CROYDON TO LONDON BRIDGE – SCHEDULE 15 MINS

Run No.	4					5				6			
Date	1st March 1967					10th March 1967				18th April 1967			
Units	4LAV 2947+2 X 4LAVs=12LAV					2 BIL 2620+2 HAL+ 2 X 4LAV=12				4 LAV 2926+ 2 X 4 LAV=12 LAV			
Driver	Not recorded					Not recorded				Not recorded			
	miles	time	mins	secs	speed	time	mins	secs	speed	time	mins	secs	speed
East Croydon	0.00	2L	00	00		1½ L	00	00		1½ L	00	00	
Windmill Bridge Jct	0.50		01	05	41		00	58	41		00	55	41½
Norwood Junction	1.67		02	34	54		02	29	53		02	31	53
MP 8¼	2.11		03	06	55		03	00	55		02	59	54½
Anerley	2.77		03	48	56		03	41	57		03	45	56
Penge West	3.17		04	14	59		04	08	58½		04	13	59
Sydenham	3.86		04	58	62		04	43	62½		04	56	61½
Forest Hill	4.73		05	45	63		05	37	63		05	45	63
MP 5½	4.86		05	54	64½		05	46	62		05	53	64
Honor Oak Park	5.62		06	34	72		06	26	66		06	33	70
MP 4	6.36		07	11	74½		07	06	70		07	10	73
Brockley	6.66		07	24	78		07	20	73		07	24	75
MP 3½	6.86		07	34	80		07	31	74½		07	34	76
New Cross Gate	7.48		07	58	*61		07	59	67		08	06	*60
Bricklayers Arms Jct	8.71		08	53	*47		08	51	*48		08	59	*51
Spa Road	9.21		10	20	53/*30 sigs		10	06	50½		10	07	56
London Bridge	10.36	½ E	12	36		1½ E	12	24		1½ E	11	59	
	net time 12 mins					net time 12½ mins				net time 12 mins			
	* brakes/speed restriction												

449 pm EAST CROYDON TO LONDON BRIDGE – SCHEDULE 15 MINS

Run No.	7					8				9			
Date	19 April 1967					23 May 1967				24 May 1967			
Units	4 LAV 2927+ 4 SUB 4715+ 4 LAV 2928= 12					4 LAVs 2939+2954+2941= 12 LAV				4 SUB 4689+ 4 LAVs 2923+2935=12			
Driver	Not recorded					James, Reigate				James, Reigate			
	miles	time	mins	secs	speed	time	mins	secs	speed	time	mins	secs	speed
East Croydon	0.00	3½ L	00	00		1½ L	00	00		T	00	00	
Windmill Bridge Jct	0.50		00	58	41½		01	04	41½		01	06	40½
Norwood Junction	1.67		02	24	54		02	31	53		02	34	53½
MP 8¼	2.11		02	56	56		03	02	55½		03	06	56
Anerley	2.77		03	36	58½		03	43	58		03	45	58½
Penge West	3.17		04	02	61		04	09	60		04	13	61
Sydenham	3.86		04	44	63		04	52	63		04	53	64½
Forest Hill	4.73		05	31	64½		05	38	64		05	40	65
MP 5½	4.86		05	39	65		05	46	65½		05	48	66
Honor Oak Park	5.62		06	18	71½		06	25	70		06	28	70
MP 4	6.36		06	55	78		07	03	74		07	06	74
Brockley	6.66		07	08	*72		07	16	76		07	19	76
MP 3½	6.86		07	21	*61		07	27	77½		07	30	75
New Cross Gate	7.48		07	54	64		07	54	*66		07	59	*64
Bricklayers Arms Jct	8.71		08	48	*50		08	45	*55		08	50	*53½
Spa Road	9.21		10	01	53½		09	48	60		09	59	56½/*9 sigs
London Bridge	10.36	½ L	11	54		1½ E	11	48		2½ E	12	23	
	net time 11¾ mins					net time 11¾ mins				net time 11¾ mins			
	* brakes/speed restriction												

miles which produced all the excitement with the right drivers on the 4.49. In those days there were no missing or misplaced mileposts, which unfortunately cannot be said today when there is barely one correctly placed post over the whole of this stretch, many having gone missing and/or been replaced with modern posts in the wrong places.

The tables show a selection of my best runs and a remarkable degree of consistency is apparent. As can be seen the train wasn't always pure 12 LAV formation; quite often a 4 SUB was substituted and on one occasion a BIL plus HAL, but always it was twelve cars.

Run 1 shows that the inclusion of a SUB did nothing to slow down progress; indeed the 80 max below Brockley was one of the highest I recorded on this train. It wasn't a case of the LAVs pulling the SUB along either as I timed a lone SUB at this speed and location the following year. Run 2 was to prove to be my fastest ever time from East Croydon to London Bridge and stands well in the RPS database against far more modern 319s, as against this 1933 built stock with 275 hp traditional traction motors and control gear. The running was typical with a steady start and no doubt the controller held right round against the stop until what would today be regarded as very late braking for the curve through New Cross Gate and the speed restriction at Bricklayers Arms Junction. Run 2 also contains my highest speed on this stretch with a multiple unit of any sort, 82mph, and a very fast finish indeed quite impossible to emulate in today's environment.

Run 3 also contained an 80 but had signal checks approaching the terminus, probably as a result if us being late and out of course. Run 4 was also another 80mph run, showing that it wasn't just Driver James who had the monopoly of these. 2947 was the only LAV unit to suffer damage from bombing in the war. Run 5 was the run where the formation included a BIL and a HAL unit and was slightly below par for the course. Run 6 was a sub 12 minute run with no real fireworks but Run 7 gave me my fastest start to pass Brockley and also included a SUB in the formation. Run 8 was pure James on 12 LAV and yet another sub 12 minute run with another very fast finish and to round off, Run 9, with another SUB in the formation, was just typical but with a maximum of 'only' 76mph.

In July 1967 steam out of Waterloo ended. I usually finished work later and I then soon married and moved to Ashford in Kent so ending this interesting and exciting spell of train timing. I hope that these runs show that the LAVS could produce some sparkling performances rather than just plodding around the Southern metals on semi-fast and stopping services.

26 May1963. 2933+2930 on up Brighton stopper at Coulsdon North, 9.39 am.

Chapter Sixteen

Snowdown Colliery – The Final Years

Snowdown, 6 April 1976. *St Thomas* on the left and *St Dunstan* on the right.

"Steam ceased to work around 1977 and the colliery closed ten years later in 1987"

Snowdown, 28 April 1973. Avonside No 2004 *St Dunstan*.

After the end of steam on the national rail network steam operation lingered on in a number of industrial locations for some years. One of these was Snowdown Colliery in Kent, which wasn't far from where we lived at Ashford in the 1970s. With the benefit of an official visitor's pass we were able to gain full access on 28 April 1973 and were pleased to find all four of the Colliery's steam locos present, even if none were actually working as activity was at a low level. In addition the two diesel shunters were there, one dumped and one working.

The table shows the engines present on that day. Of the steam engines, three were built by the Avonside Engine Company in Bristol in 1927 and two of these have survived into preservation. Number 2004, 0-6-0 saddle tank *St Dunstan* which was standing in light steam outside the shed on the day of our visit, is preserved, appropriately, on the East Kent Railway just a short distance away at Shepherds Well.

St Dunstan is now the subject of a lottery appeal by the East Kent Railway to restore it to full working order. The second Avonside, 1971 *St Thomas*,

SNOWDOWN COLLIERY – 28 APRIL 1973

LOCOMOTIVES PRESENT

0-6-0DL Andrew Barclay No 382 of 1950. Out of Use
0-4-0DM John Fowler No 416002 of 1952. In Use
Hunslet 0-6-0ST No 3825 of 1954. Boiler washout
Avonside 0-6-0ST No 2004 of 1927. *St Dunstan*. In Use
Avonside 0-6-0ST No 1971 of 1927. *St Thomas*. Workshop
Avonside 0-6-0ST No ? of 1927 *St Martin*. Dumped

28 April 1973. Avonside No 2004 *St Dunstan* outside the shed with Hunslet No 3825 just visible inside.

28 April 1973. Hunslet 3825 inside shed for boiler washout.

is preserved at the Dover Transport Museum. This engine was lurking inside the shed during our visit. The third, *St Martin*, was dumped out in the open and subsequently scrapped. The fourth steam engine was Hunslet 0-6-0 saddle tank 3825 built in 1954 and this was having a boiler washout. It currently resides on the Stainmore Railway at Kirby Stephen East as BR 68009, many miles from home. Of the two diesel shunters, 0-4-0DM, John Fowler 416002 of 1952 was in use and is also preserved at the East Kent Railway. The other, Andrew Barclay 0-6-0 DL Number 382 built in 1950 was dumped out of use next to *St Martin*. I have been unable to trace its fate. A subsequent visit on 6 April 1976 saw Hunslet 3825 working and two of the Avonsides, *St Thomas* and *St Dunstan* dead outside the shed. Neither diesel was to be seen. Steam ceased to work around 1977 and the colliery closed ten years later in 1987.

Snowdown, 6 April 1976. All three operational steam engines in the yard.

28 April 1973. Avonside 0-6-0ST *St Dunstan*.

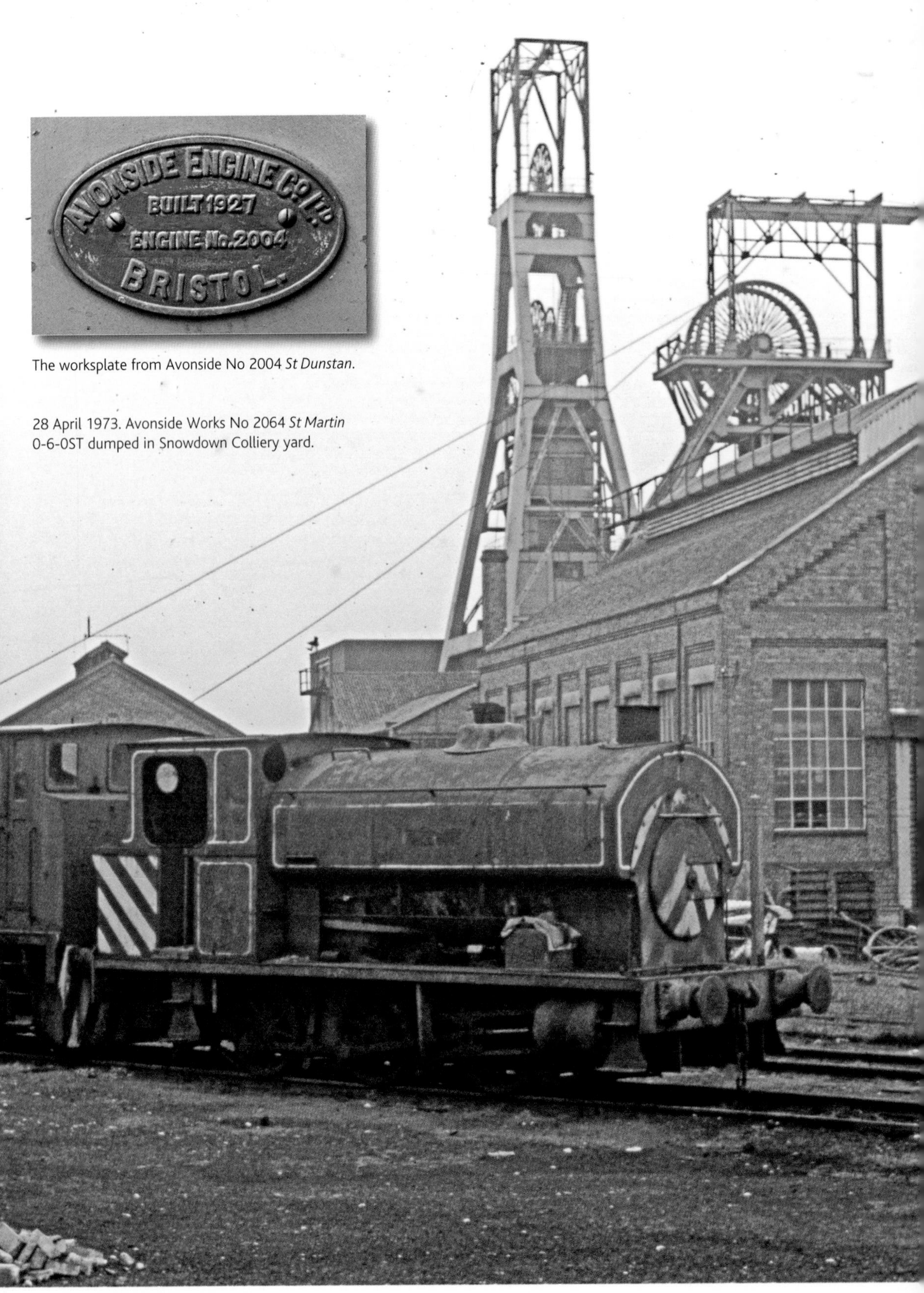

The worksplate from Avonside No 2004 *St Dunstan*.

28 April 1973. Avonside Works No 2064 *St Martin* 0-6-0ST dumped in Snowdown Colliery yard.

Snowdown, 28 April 1973. Dumped Avonside *St Martin* with Barclay DM 382.

29 July 2007. *St Dunstan* on the East Kent Railway. On the left Cep unit 7105 with buffet car from Bep 7014.

Chapter Seventeen

Basingstoke to Woking

7 May 2015. 444.018 at Woking with a Weymouth to Waterloo train.

"Not that much faster than steam went all those years ago, but oh so much easier to do!"

23 May 1964. 34019 *Bideford* entering Woking on the 8.46 am Salisbury to Waterloo.

One or two recent fast and unchecked runs on the Basingstoke to Woking section on South West trains' orderly empire prompted me to look back over the years to see how the quietly competent 444 Desiros compare to past traction and how much progress has actually been made in start to stop times over this favourite racing stretch of mine. (The answer to this question is 'not much'). Timing trains out of Waterloo started for me in 1960 though it wasn't until 1964 that I acquired a decent stop watch and therefore produced logs which can be relied on, with some exceptions in 1962 when I was travelling with a suitably equipped friend. GPS was of course a long way off and in fact I still don't use it much on SWT as the window coating on the Desiros and on some of the 159s prevents the acquisition of a decent signal. Fortunately the tiny LSWR mileposts have largely been replaced or supplemented by large blue posts, though quite a few of these are misplaced. As far as possible the photographs are taken at Basingstoke or Woking or at points in between and show either the locomotive or unit featured in the logs or one of the same class.

So we start with Table One with Bulleid light Pacifics hauling heavy loads. And the two runs demonstrate the relative ease with which mile-a-minute runs could be achieved with decent loads, though full or nearly full regulator would have been needed. Earlier Sullivan had taken 34019 over Roundwood at a very respectable

27 June 1964. 34102 *Lapford* passing Vauxhall with the 5.54 pm Waterloo to Basingstoke local.

27 June 1964. 34001 *Exeter* passing Vauxhall on the 11 am Padstow to Waterloo.

TABLE ONE – BULLEID LIGHT PACIFICS WITH HEAVY LOADS

Date	5 December 1964						20 June 1965				
Train	1 pm Bournemouth West to Waterloo						954 am Weymouth to Waterloo				
Engine	Rebuilt WC class 4-6-2 34004 *Yeovil*						Unrebuilt WC class 4-6-2 34019 *Bideford*				
Load	12 coaches, 405 tons tare, 430 tons gross						13 coaches and 1 van, 458 tons tare, 500 tons gross				
Driver	Not known						J Sullivan Nine Elms No 3 Link				
Fireman	Not Known						A Rowe				
Position	Rear						Rear				
Weather	wet and misty turning to rain						dry and sunny				
	miles	sched	mins	secs	speed		sched	mins	secs	speed	
Basingstoke	0.00	0.00	00	00		14 late	0.00	00	00		25 late
Newnham Siding (Site)	4.10		05	59	61			05	54	64½	slow line
Hook	5.59		07	27	65			07	14	69	
Winchfield	7.92		09	35	70½			09	17	73	
Fleet	11.27		12	20	75/77			11	57	76/77	
Farnborough	14.55		14	53	76			14	34	70*	brakes
Sturt Lane	15.60		15	45	75			15	28	68½	
MP 31	16.75		16	43	73½			16	32	66½	
Pirbright Junction	18.26		17	51	77½/79			17	44	71	
Brookwood	19.76		19	04	78	eased		19	04	74½	
Woking Junction	23.00		21	51	53*	brakes		22	35	0*	sigs stop
								23	15		
Woking	23.46	26.00	22	47		11 late	35.00	25	05		15 late
	start to stop average 61.78mph						net time 22¾ mins start to stop average Basingstoke to sigs stop 61.10mph				

11 April 1964. 34004 *Yeovil* passing Woking at speed with an up Ocean Liner Express.

30 March 1964. Fireman Les Hoath awaits the right away from Woking on 34009 *Lyme Regis* working the 9.30 am Waterloo to Bournemouth.

TABLE TWO – HIGH SPEED LIGHT PACIFICS

Date	16 June 1966	29 December 1966
Train	635 pm Salisbury to Waterloo	635 pm Salisbury to Waterloo
Engine	Rebuilt WC class 4-6-2 34009 *Lyme Regis*	Bulleid unrebuilt BB class 4-6-2 34057 *Biggin Hill*
Load	4 coaches and 5 vans, 260 tons tare, 280 tons gross	4 coaches and 2 vans, 179 tons tare, 185 tons gross
Driver	L Cummings Nine Elms No 3 link	Jim Evans, Nine Elms No 2 Link
Position	Rear	Rear
Weather		cold and dark

	miles	sched	mins	secs	speed		miles	sched	mins	secs	speed	
Basingstoke	0.00	0.00	00	00		3 late	0.00	0.00	00	00		8 late
MP 46	1.75		02	58	62½		1.75		02	52	63	
Newnham Siding (Site)	4.10		04	55	76		4.10		04	47	82½	
Hook	5.59		06	04	82		5.59		05	52	86	
MP 41	6.75		06	56	84		6.75		06	42	89	
Winchfield	7.92		07	44	87		7.92		07	32	93	
MP 38	9.75		08	59	93		9.75		08	43	90	brakes
Fleet	11.27		09	57	92/93		11.27		09	48	84	
MP 35	12.75		10	54	90		12.75		10	52	88	
Farnborough	14.55		12	10	86		14.55		12	03	86½	
Sturt Lane	15.60		12	54	87		15.60		12	47	88	
MP 31	16.75		13	43	86		16.75		13	38	84	
Pirbright Junction	18.26		14	40	90/91		18.26		14	39	86	
Brookwood	19.76		15	44	90		19.76		15	46	87½	
MP 27	20.75		16	26	84		20.75		16	28	83	
Woking Junction	23.00		18	56	*39/50	sigs	23.00		18	26	55	
Woking	23.46	28.00	19	48		5 early	23.46	28.00	19	14		1 early

	net time 19 minutes start to stop average 71.09mph	Mainly done on 160lbs of steam and 20% cut off start to stop average 73.19mph

Date	24 May 1967	14 June 1967
Train	615 pm Weymouth to Waterloo	635 pm Salisbury to Waterloo
Engine	Bulleid rebuilt WC 4-6-2 34001 *Exeter*	Bulleid unrebuilt WC 4-6-2 34102 *Lapford*
Load	3 coaches and 6 vans*, 239½ tons tare, 260 tons gross	5 coaches and 2 vans*, 214 tons tare, 235 tons gross
Driver	Jim Evans, Nine Elms No 2 Link	J Gaffney, Nine Elms No 4 Link
Fireman	C Arbuckle	R Lee
Position	Rear	Rear
Weather	Heavy rain	Fine and warm, light SW wind

	miles	sched	mins	secs	speed		miles	sched	mins	secs	speed	
Basingstoke	0.00	0.00	00	00		R/time	0.00	0.00	00	00		2 late
MP 46	1.75		03	08	61½		1.75		03	09	55½	
Newnham Siding (Site)	4.10		05	08	75½		4.10		05	18	73	
Hook	5.59		06	19	80		5.59		06	28	83	
MP 41	6.75		07	13	82		6.75		07	18	87	
Winchfield	7.92		08	06	84		7.92		08	05	92	
MP 38	9.75		09	21	89		9.75		09	15	98/97	
Fleet	11.27		10	22	87½		11.27		10	10	98½	
MP 35	12.75		11	23	90		12.75		11	05	100	
Farnborough	14.55		12	36	83		14.55		12	31	64*	brakes
Sturt Lane	15.60		13	22	85		15.60		13	34	53*	pws
MP 31	16.75		14	14	84		16.75		14	54	58½	
Pirbright Junction	18.26		15	11	90		18.26		16	06	76	
Brookwood	19.76		16	13	94		19.76		17	16	88	
MP 27	20.75		16	52	83	brakes	20.75		17	57	83	brakes
Woking Junction	23.00		18	49	63		23.00		20	37	*47/50	sigs
Woking	23.46	26.00	19	34		7 early	23.46	28.00	21	30		4 early

	* including 75mph vans (2) start to stop average 71.94mph	net time 18¾ *including a 75mph van start to stop average 65.47mph MP38-MP35=98.2mph

55mph from the Winchester start.

Table Two is a selection of my many high speed dashes with light Pacifics with fairly light loads and shows just what steam could achieve. There is no doubt in my mind that a 20 minute booking would have been practical with engines in their prime but the fact is that these times were all set toward the end of steam with run down engines. The run with *Lyme Regis* in particular required very little effort. The *Lapford* run though was a very different proposition as John (Boy) Gaffney set out to try for the 'ton' and just achieved it, after Bramshott at the foot of the half mile of 1 in 655 down. The noise was absolutely incredible with the engine being worked in full regulator and 40 per cent cut off. This run has also appeared elsewhere with a maximum speed shown of less than 100mph. However I knew this stretch of line like the back of my hand and had a set routine always taking readings at the same quarter mileposts to ensure both consistency and to avoid the misplaced posts. My milepost readings fully support the speeds shown.

Table Three shows some good, competent runs behind BR Standard class 5s with reasonable loads plus one of a couple I had with a Standard Class 4 2-6-0 on quite a good load. Salisbury could and did turnout almost anything for the 6.35 pm up, but 76066 was a little underpowered so this was a good effort.

And finally with steam in Table Four one of the high speed Merchant Navy efforts in 1967. This shows that the current

11 June 1964. Standard 5 73171 near Wimbledon on the 7.02 pm Clapham Junction to Eastleigh vans.

TABLE THREE – BR STANDARDS

Date	14 June1966	10 August 1066
Train	635 pm Salisbury to Waterloo	635 pm Salisbury to Waterloo
Engine	BR Standard Class 5 4-6-0 73171	BR Standard Class 5 4-6-0 73088
Load	5 coaches and 6 vans, 304 tons tare, 325 tons gross	6 coaches and 6 vans 303 tons tare, 325 tons gross
Driver	L Cummings Nine Elms No 3 link	Ball Nine Elms No 3 link
Position	Rear	Rear
Weather	-	-

	miles	sched	mins	secs	speed		miles	sched	mins	secs	speed	
Basingstoke	0.00	0.00	00	00		4 late	0.00	0.00	00	00		10 late
MP 46	1.75		03	26	50		1.75		03	11	55½	
Newnham Siding (Site)	4.10		05	53	60/59		4.10		05	26	65	
Hook	5.59		07	25	62½		5.59		06	47	70½	
MP 41	6.75		08	32	64		6.75		07	46	72	
Winchfield	7.92		09	38	67		7.92		08	44	74½	
MP 38	9.75		11	12	71½		9.75		10	10	79½	
Fleet	11.27		12	30	70		11.27		11	18	79	
MP 35	12.75		13	47	71		12.75		12	27	78	
Farnborough	14.55		15	16	68		14.55		13	49	74	
Sturt Lane	15.60		16	10	69		15.60		14	40	73	
MP 31	16.75		17	14	67		16.75		15	41	70	
Pirbright Junction	18.26		18	25	72½		18.26		16	54	71	
Brookwood	19.76		19	44	74½		19.76		18	15	73	
MP 27	20.75		20	33	73		20.75		19	05	74	
Woking Junction	23.00		22	36	60*	brakes	23.00		21	42	*38/43½	sigs
Woking	23.46	28.00	23	20		r/t	23.46	28.00	22	48		5 late
	start to stop average 60.33mph						net time 22 minutes start to stop average 61.74mph					

Date	15 June 1967	2 January 1967
Train	635 pm Salisbury to Waterloo	635 pm Salisbury to Waterloo
Engine	BR Standard Class 5 4-6-0 73029	BR Standard Class 4 2-6-0 76066
Load	5 coaches and 2 vans, 214 tons tare, 235 tons gross	8 coaches and 2 vans, 327 tons tare, 345 tons gross
Driver	J Gaffney, Nine Elms No 4 Link	JJ Smith, Nine Elms No 4 Link
Fireman	T Moult	
Position	Rear	Rear
Weather	Fine and warm, light SW wind	Cold and dark

	miles	sched	mins	secs	speed		miles	sched	mins	secs	speed	
Basingstoke	0.00	0.00	00	00		2 late	0.00	0.00	00	00		14 late
MP 46	1.75		02	44	63		1.75		03	36	49	
Newnham Siding (Site)	4.10		04	41	75½		4.10		06	14	56½/55	
Hook	5.59		05	54	77		5.59		07	50	57½	
MP 41	6.75		06	48	78½		6.75		09	06	56	
Winchfield	7.92		07	42	80		7.92		10	22	58	
MP 38	9.75		09	04	82½		9.75		12	10	64½	
Fleet	11.27		10	11	80		11.27		13	36	62	
MP 35	12.75		11	20	76		12.75		15	6	60	
Farnborough	14.55		12	51	63*	brakes	14.55		16	57	54	
Sturt Lane	15.60		13	54	58*	pws	15.60		18	11	55½	
MP 31	16.75		15	04	63½		16.75		19	31	54	
Pirbright Junction	18.26		16	16	73		18.26		21	00	60	
Brookwood	19.76		17	53	47*	sigs	19.76		22	33	64/65½	
MP 27	20.75		18	51	66/74½		20.75		23	30	63	
Woking Junction	23.00		20	46	65		23.00		25	56	51	
Woking	23.46	28.00	21	39		4 early	23.46	28.00	26	50		13 late
	net time 20 minutes start to stop average 65.02mph											

20 June 1964. 73088 at Basingstoke on the 12.53 pm local to Waterloo.

13 July 1963. 76017 approaching Woking with the 1.01 pm Salisbury to Waterloo stopping service.

TABLE FOUR – HIGH SPEED MERCHANTS

Date	25 May 1967
Train	615 pm Weymouth to Waterloo
Engine	Bulleid rebuilt MN 4-6-2 35023 *Holland Africa Line*
Load	3 coaches and 5 vans*, 243 tons tare, 265 tons gross
Driver	A Fordrey, Nine Elms No 1 Link
Fireman	Cottee
Position	Rear
Weather	Dry and warm, but wet rails

	miles	sched	mins	secs	speed	
Basingstoke	0.00	0.00	00	00		2 late
MP 46	1.75		03	05	60½	
Newnham Siding (Site)	4.10		05	08	73	
Hook	5.59		06	20	80	
MP 41	6.75		07	14	82½	
Winchfield	7.92		08	04	87	
MP 38	9.75		09	17	94/93	
Fleet	11.27		10	14	94/95	
MP 35	12.75		11	13	91	
Farnborough	14.55		12	32	78*	brakes
Sturt Lane	15.60		13	18	82	
MP 31	16.75		14	12	84	
Pirbright Junction	18.26		15	08	90	
Brookwood	19.76		16	10	96	
MP 27	20.75		16	48	93	
Woking Junction	23.00		19	34	*38/44	sigs
Woking	23.46	26.00	20	36		4 early

net time 19¼ minutes
* incl a 75mph van
start to stop average 68.33mph

Date	27 June 1967
Train	615 pm Weymouth to Waterloo
Engine	Bulleid rebuilt MN class 4-6-2 35028 *Clan Line*
Load	3 coaches and 4 vans*, 205½ tons tare, 220 tons gross
Driver	F Burridge, Nine Elms No 3 Link
Fireman	Simon
Position	Rear
Weather	damp, wet rails, calm

	miles	sched	mins	secs	speed	
Basingstoke	0.00	0.00	00	00		6 late
MP 46	1.75		02	47	64	
Newnham Siding (Site)	4.10		04	42	80	
Hook	5.59		05	48	83	
MP 41	6.75		06	37	87½	
Winchfield	7.92		07	26	90	slipping
MP 38	9.75		08	37	93	
Fleet	11.27		09	34	95	
MP 35	12.75		10	32	93	slipping
Farnborough	14.55		11	45	82	
Sturt Lane	15.60		12	33	59*	pws
MP 31	16.75		13	44	64½	
Pirbright Junction	18.26		14	52	80	
Brookwood	19.76		16	00	88½	
MP 27	20.75		16	42	84	
Woking Junction	23.00		18	34	63	
Woking	23.46	26.00	19	24		R/T

net time 18½ mins
* incl a 75mph van
start to stop average 72.56mph

DMU and EMU bookings could have been kept with steam. And that's with the condition that these engines were in by the end. There were a number of runs over this stretch where the Merchant Navy Pacifics reached and exceeded 100mph and these are dealt with in my forthcoming book on the untold story of the last two years of steam on the Southern.

Table Five shows some runs with the immediate replacements for steam, the innovative REPs and TCs, which were a good solution at the time but only because the extra cost of electrification right through to Weymouth couldn't be justified. For many years the first run in Table Five was my fastest on this stretch though I didn't venture into this part of the world so much in the years following the end of steam due to marriage and then work commitments. The REPS were fine units and could produce some lightning accelerations if working with just the single TC unit.

Then we had the Warship era on the Exeters, followed in the late 1980s by the magnificent Class 50s with the Type 3 'Cromptons' on some of the semi-fasts. Most of the latter were push-pull with a single TC unit, but my favourite trains were the two which had MK 1 stock and decent loads. What can one say about the 50s? They were superb machines capable of very fast running and starts to rival the EMUs. The run with 50.023 benefitted by having one coach less than normal and turned in a net time equal to my fastest with a 444, and twenty-five years separate these forms of motive power! They were however non-standard and unreliable so didn't last.

Then came the class 73 EDLs during the transition period when the REP traction motors were being taken to be used in the new 442s and some interesting train formations could be found. The run in Table Six was nine coaches, including a 5 car TCB buffet set with the two 73s

3 June 1963. 35028 *Clan Line* near Pirbright with the 9.21 am Weymouth to Waterloo.

28 February 1986. REP 3005 leading TC418 on the 9 am Bournemouth to Waterloo approaching Basingstoke.

TABLE FIVE – RPSs

Date	16 October 1967						14 July 1968				
Train	644 pm Weymouth to Waterloo						346pm Bournemouth to Waterloo				
Units	REP 3008+4TC						REP3010+TC425+TC428				
Driver	Hutchinson						Elliot				
Position	In 3008						In TC428				
Weather	windy										
	miles	sched	mins	secs	speed		sched	mins	secs	speed	
Basingstoke	0.00	0.00	00	00		31 late	0.00	00	00		2 late
MP 46	1.75		02	14	80			02	20	74	
Newnham Siding (Site)	4.10		03	49	95			04	02	87	
Hook	5.59		04	42	99			05	04	90/87	
MP 41	6.75		05	26	100			05	53	89	
Winchfield	7.92		06	10	101			06	40	92	
MP 38	9.75		07	12	106/104			07	50	97	
Fleet	11.27		08	03	105			08	47	90	brakes
MP 35	12.75		08	55	103			09	50	85	
Farnborough	14.55		10	04	*86½	brakes		11	01	89	
Sturt Lane	15.60		10	46	92			11	53	90	
MP 31	16.75		11	33	94			12	33	88/90	
Pirbright Junction	18.26		12	25	100			13	30	88/87	
Brookwood	19.76		13	26	91			14	35	89	
MP 27	20.75		14	08	85			15	16	86½	
Woking Junction	23.00		15	54	64*	brakes		17	03	63*	brakes
Woking	23.46	19.30	16	46		28 late	19.30	17	48		R/T
	start to stop average 83.96mph				MP 38-35 =104.85mph		start to stop average 79.08mph				

Date	14 December 1968					
Train	1244 pm Weymouth to Waterloo					
Units	REP3002+TC420					
Position	In TC420					
	miles	sched	mins	secs	speed	
Basingstoke	0.00	0.00	00	00		R/T
MP 46	1.75		02	05	80½	
Newnham Siding (Site)	4.10		03	40	92	
Hook	5.59		04	36	97	
MP 41	6.75		05	22	90	
Winchfield	7.92		06	10	95	
MP 38	9.75		07	16	98½	
Fleet	11.27		08	13	93	
MP 35	12.75		09	11	98	
Farnborough	14.55		10	21	90	
Sturt Lane	15.60		11	04	91	
MP 31	16.75		11	53	90	
Pirbright Junction	18.26		12	45	98	
Brookwood	19.76		13	43	103	
MP 27	20.75		14	18	100	
Woking Junction	23.00		17	03	23*	sigs
Woking	23.46	19.30	17	50		2 early
	net time 16¾ minutes start to stop average 78.93mph					

OPPOSITE:
10 March 1988. 33.110 near Pirbright with the 7.16 am Salisbury to Waterloo.

22 April 1988. 50.018 at Old Basing with the 5.50 am Exeter to Waterloo.

62

TABLE SIX – DLs and EDLs

Date	20 October 1986	1 October 1988
Train	1315 Salisbury to Waterloo	1046 Bournemouth to Waterloo
Engine	Class 33/1 B-B 33.116	Class 73 B-Bs 73.132+73.136
Load	8 coaches and 2 vans, 334 tons tare, 345 tons gross	5TCB 2804+4TC 8036 320 tons gross
Position	Rear	Rear
Weather		dry and sunny

	miles	sched	mins	secs	speed		sched	mins	secs	speed	
Basingstoke	0.00	0.00	00	00		1 late		00	00		from sigs stop
MP 46	1.75		02	54	57			02	45	70½	
Newnham Siding (Site)	4.10		04	59	70½			04	26	84	
Hook	5.59		06	16	73			05	26	88	
MP 41	6.75		07	14	75			06	16	92	
Winchfield	7.92		08	10	78			07	00	93	
MP 38	9.75		09	31	82½			08	11	95	
Fleet	11.27		10	37	82			09	06	96	
MP 35	12.75		11	43	84			10	03	97	
Farnborough	14.55		13	01	82			11	10	92	
Sturt Lane	15.60		13	46	81			11	52	93	
MP 31	16.75		14	41	78			12	39	90	
Pirbright Junction	18.26		15	42	82			13	33	95	
Brookwood	19.76		16	53	83			14	31	98	
MP 27	20.75		17	37	80			15	09	90	brakes
Woking Junction	23.00		20	59	*22/30	pws		17	34	*44/60	sigs
Woking	23.46	22.00	21	54		1 late		17	57	63	pass

	net time 20½ minutes start to stop average 64.27mph	equivalent start to stop 17½ minutes MP41-MP27=94.56mph

Date	6 November 1987
Train	1220 Exeter St Davids to Waterloo
Engine	Class 50 Co-Co 50.023 *Howe*
Load	8 coaches (MK2 a-c), 262½ tons tare, 280 tons gross
Position	Rear
Weather	fog

	miles	sched	mins	secs	speed	
Basingstoke	0.00	0.00	00	00		1 late
MP 46	1.75		02	25	68½	
Newnham Siding (Site)	4.10		04	11	83	
Hook	5.59		05	12	88½	
MP 41	6.75		06	01	91	
Winchfield	7.92		06	45	96	
MP 38	9.75		07	53	100	
Fleet	11.27		08	46	102	
MP 35	12.75		09	39	104	
Farnborough	14.55		10	40	102	
Sturt Lane	15.60		11	17	103	
MP 31	16.75		12	00	100	
Pirbright Junction	18.26		12	47	104	
Brookwood	19.76		14	07	63*	sigs
MP 27	20.75		14	55	77½	
Woking Junction	23.00		17	04	27*	sigs
Woking	23.46	19.30	18	17		R/T

net time 16½ minutes
start to stop average 77.0mph MP38-MP31=102.03mph

OPPOSITE:
27 September 1987. 33.051 near Old Basing with the 10.05 am Southampton Docks to Waterloo QE2 Ocean Liner Express.

10 March 1988. 33.119 on the 8.10 am Waterloo to Salisbury.

96

62

20 April 2005. Class 442 No 2415 on the 15.05 pm Waterloo to Poole at Winchester.

TABLE SEVEN – 442s

Date	30 November 2006					10 January 2007			
Train	1418 Winchester to Waterloo					1318 Winchester to Waterloo			
Units	2411					2422			
Position	5/5					5/5			
Weather	cloudy					sunny periods			
	miles	mins	secs	speed		mins	secs	speed	
Basingstoke	0.00	00	00		R/T	00	00		R/T
MP 46	1.75	02	44	74½	slow line	02	09	79	
Newnham Siding (Site)	4.10	04	24	86/82		03	43	94/93	
Hook	5.59	05	27	86½		04	39	96	
MP 41	6.75	06	20	83		05	25	94	
Winchfield	7.92	07	09	87		06	10	94	
MP 38	9.75	08	24	83		07	19	96	
Fleet	11.27	09	28	86½		08	17	95	
MP 35	12.75	-	-	53*	sigs	09	14	96	
Farnborough	14.55	12	47	37*	fast line	10	20	95	
Sturt Lane	15.60	14	19	58½		10	57	96	
MP 31	16.75	15	21	72½		11	44	96	
Pirbright Junction	18.26	16	20	90		12	37	98	
Brookwood	19.76	17	24	97		13	37	96½	
MP 27	20.75	18	06	94		14	14	97	
Woking Junction	23.00	19	29	92		17	18	*30/40	sigs
Woking	23.46	19	44	93	pass	17	46	54	pass
	equivalent start to stop time 17¾ minutes					equivalent start to stop time 17¾ minutes			

22 April 1988. 73.129 at Old Basing on the 6.54 am Bournemouth to Waterloo.

TABLE EIGHT – MK 1 EMUs

Date	14 May 2004					22 November 2004			
Train	1548 Winchester to Waterloo					1448 Winchester to Waterloo			
Units	1316+2315 ('Greyhound' CIG+'Greyhound' CEP)					1313+1319 (both 'Greyhound' CIGs)			
Position	Rear					Rear			
Weather	fine and warm								
	miles	mins	secs	speed		mins	secs	speed	
Basingstoke	0.00	00	00		2 late	00	00		R/T
MP 46	1.75	02	38	70½		02	11	76½	
Newnham Siding (Site)	4.10	04	23	82		03	49	88	
Hook	5.59	05	24	88		04	50	84	
MP 41	6.75	06	13	90		05	41	86½	
Winchfield	7.92	06	59	93		06	30	92	
MP 38	9.75	08	09	98		07	38	98	
Fleet	11.27	09	04	97		08	37	83*	brakes
MP 35	12.75	09	59	99		09	41	87/90	
Farnborough	14.55	11	05	97		10	53	83*	brakes
Sturt Lane	15.60	11	43	99		11	38	86½	
MP 31	16.75	12	28	96		12	28	84	
Pirbright Junction	18.26	13	19	100		13	26	86½	
Brookwood	19.76	14	19	95		14	31	92	
MP 27	20.75	14	56	97		15	11	88	
Woking Junction	23.00	-	-	23*	sigs	17	18	*51/60	sigs
Woking	23.46	18	41	47	pass	17	38	71	pass
	equivalent start to stop 17¼ minutes MP41-MP27=96.38mph					equivalent start to stop 17½ minutes MP41-MP27=88.42mph			

Date	4 December 2004				
Train	1448 Winchester to Waterloo				
Units	1315+3456 ('Greyhound' CIG+VEP)				
Position	4/8				
	miles	mins	secs	speed	
Basingstoke	0.00	00	00		R/T
MP 46	1.75	02	12	75½	
Newnham Siding (Site)	4.10	03	51	86	
Hook	5.59	04	53	90	
MP 41	6.75	05	41	91	
Winchfield	7.92	06	29	93	
MP 38	9.75	07	39	95	
Fleet	11.27	08	38	88½	
MP 35	12.75	09	39	90	
Farnborough	14.55	10	49	92	
Sturt Lane	15.60	11	31	91	
MP 31	16.75	12	19	90	
Pirbright Junction	18.26	13	10	97	
Brookwood	19.76	14	16	86½	
MP 27	20.75	14	59	80	
Woking Junction	23.00	18	28	23*	sigs
Woking	23.46	19	28	49	
	equivalent start to stop 17¼ minutes MP41-MP27=90.32mph				

OPPOSITE:
12 December 2006. Class 442 No 2405 on the 11.05 am Waterloo to Poole passing Woking.

24 March 2005. Greyhound CEP 2315 leaving Basingstoke with the 11.09 am Waterloo to Portsmouth Harbour.

2315
2315
8
CAR STOP
9

TABLE NINE – DMUs

Date	16 September 2006						14 March 2007				
Train	1345 Salisbury to Waterloo						1320 Salisbury to Waterloo				
Units	170.308						159.012				
Position	2/2	stop watch					3/3	stop watch			
Weather	cloudy						sunny periods				
	miles	sched	mins	secs	speed		sched	mins	secs	speed	
Basingstoke	0.00	0.00	00	00		R/T	0.00	00	00		R/T
MP 46	1.75		02	21	71			02	20	71½	
Newnham Siding (Site)	4.10		04	04	88			04	01	90	
Hook	5.59		05	01	92			04	58	93	
MP 41	6.75		05	48	93			05	46	88	
Winchfield	7.92		06	33	94			06	34	93	
MP 38	9.75		07	43	96			07	46	91	
Fleet	11.27		08	40	92			08	46	88½	
MP 35	12.75		09	40	90			09	46	91	
Farnborough	14.55		10	55	85			10	55	91	
Sturt Lane	15.60		11	39	84			11	36	92	
MP 31	16.75		12	32	78			12	25	90	
Pirbright Junction	18.26		13	32	81			13	19	93	
Brookwood	19.76		14	44	86			14	22	94	
MP 27	20.75		15	26	86			15	00	93	
Woking Junction	23.00		18	11	33*	sigs		17	14	*26/55	sigs
Woking	23.46	18.00	19	15		1 late	18.00	17	59		R/T
	net time 18 minutes MP41-MP27= 87.20mph						net time 17½ minutes MP41-MP27=90.98mph				

Date	30 June 2011					
Train	0641 Exeter to Waterloo					
Units	159.022+159.106					
Position	6/6	stop watch				
Weather	Warm, sunny periods					
	miles	sched	mins	secs	speed	
Basingstoke	0.00	0.00	00	00		1 late
MP 46	1.75		02	33	72½	
Newnham Siding (Site)	4.10		04	15	91	
Hook	5.59		05	15	86½	
MP 41	6.75		06	03	88	
Winchfield	7.92		06	51	86½	
MP 38	9.75		08	06	89	
Fleet	11.27		09	07	87	
MP 35	12.75		10	09	86½	
Farnborough	14.55		11	18	87	
Sturt Lane	15.60		11	57	88	
MP 31	16.75		12	54	86½/90	
Pirbright Junction	18.26		13	50	88	
Brookwood	19.76		14	56	86½	
MP 27	20.75		15	38	86	
Woking	23.46	18.00	18	05		1 late
	start to stop average 77.84mph Mp41-MP27=87.65mph					

OPPOSITE:
1 April 2005. CIG 1890 on arrival at Basingstoke with the 10.57 am from Brighton.

1 April 2005. VEP 3401 at Basingstoke on the 12.09 pm Waterloo to Portsmouth Harbour.

3
1890
1890
31

3401
3401
Passenger Lift to
and Platforms 1, 4
Way out
1, 4 and 5

20 April 2005. Greyhound CIG 1304 trailing the 15.51 pm Portsmouth Harbour to Waterloo at Clapham Junction.

stretching the 90mph limit for these engines and was a joy to time. This was part of a booked non-stop run from Southampton Parkway to Waterloo. The overall time was 61 minutes and 16 seconds or 56 minutes net for the 74.83 miles. Today there are no bookings anything like as fast, though in my view there ought to be.

For various reasons I didn't cover the 442 era very much, but in my opinion these units are probably the finest ever to run on Southern Rails and it's fitting that they continue in use today on the Brighton line, where they receive my attention from time to time and where they still appear to have a future post-Thameslink upgrade. Table Seven shows some runs with these fine units.

Table Eight brings us into the CIG/ CEP era, albeit at the end. The stopping pattern of the Bournemouth line trains now meant that it was quite difficult to get a train with Basingstoke and Woking stops in its journey as most of the faster services were Winchester to Woking or Basingstoke to Clapham Junction. The Greyhound units, both CIGs and CEPs had an extra stage of field weakening and so could run faster than the standard units. In theory this should not have affected the starts but seemed to nevertheless, and the time to MP 46 with 1313+1319 is amongst the fastest I have ever recorded. The 100mph at Pirbright with 1316+2315 was superb and I must

TABLE TEN – 444s

Date	17 December 2009	6 May 2011
Train	0900 Southampton Central to Waterloo	0900 Southampton Central to Waterloo
Units	444.037+444.005	444.001+444.007
Position	8/10 stop watch	7/10 stop watch
Weather	sunny periods	sunny periods

	miles	sched	mins	secs	speed		sched	mins	secs	speed	
Basingstoke	0.00	0.00	00	00		2 late	0.00	00	00		2 late
MP 46	1.75		02	17	72			02	11	74	
Newnham Siding (Site)	4.10		03	58	86½			03	47	92½	
Hook	5.59		04	57	94			04	43	99	
MP 41	6.75		05	42	97½/99½			05	28	99½/98½	
Winchfield	7.92		06	24	99			06	09	99½	
MP 38	9.75		07	30	97½/99½			07	17	99	
Fleet	11.27		08	24	98½			08	10	98½	
MP 35	12.75		09	20	98			09	06	99½	
Farnborough	14.55		10	25	99½			10	09	99½	
Sturt Lane	15.60		10	57	99½			10	48	98½	
MP 31	16.75		11	45	98			11	31	99½/98½	
Pirbright Junction	18.26		12	35	101½			12	19	100	
Brookwood	19.76		13	32	100			13	19	101	
MP 27	20.75		14	08	99½			13	55	100	
Woking Junction	23.00		15	43	62*			15	29	54*	
Woking	23.46	19.00	16	28		½ early	19.00	16	21		½ early
	start to stop average 85.49mph MP41-MP27=99.61mph						start to stop average 86.09mph MP41-MP27=99.41mph				

admit to letting out a muffled shout of joy at this at-long-last realised ambition with MK 1 EMU, only ever equalled in December of the same year with a non-Greyhound CEP on the steep downhill section at Hildenborough with the CEP Farewell Tour.

And so to the current scene which, since our move away from East Sussex to be near Southampton, has meant much easier access to trains with the Basingstoke and Woking stopping pattern. The 159s (Table Nine) perform well but the 18 minute standard booking is very tight if the 90mph limit is observed and with the usual signal check approaching Woking if running on time. Our favourite train for trips to London during the week is the 9 am from Southampton and it is this train with its 444+444 formation which has given me my two fastest Basingstoke to Woking start to stop times shown in Table Ten, the 16 minutes 21 seconds being a Railway Performance Society fastest time of recent years.

To achieve sub 16½ minutes means a fast start, preferably at least 2 minutes late and a good finish with running as close to the 100mph limit as possible, which both these runs did. I estimate that the theoretical fastest time possible within the laid down speed limit is about 16 minutes 10 seconds, not that much faster than steam went all those years ago, but oh so much easier to do!

24 March 2005. Cab of Greyhound CEP 2315 at Waterloo.

Chapter Eighteen

The 012 Pacifics

24 April 1971. 012.001 arriving at Neumünster with the 06.44 Kiel to Hamburg.

"This chapter is a tribute to the class of locomotives which I consider represented the high water mark of Pacific steam power worldwide"

24 April 1971. 012.104 at Flensburg waiting to take the 'Nord Pfeil' express to Hamburg.

The end of May 2015 marked forty years since the end of Western European express steam power in normal service, when the 012 Pacifics finally ceased to roar up and down between Rheine and Emden in northern Germany. This chapter is a tribute to the class of locomotives which I consider represented the high water mark of Pacific steam power worldwide. There were of course many claims to this position. Nobody can discount the achievements of Bulleid's superb machines or those of Gresley, Stanier or Chapelon. For their size the Bulleid Pacifics were probably unrivalled in Great Britain although the Gresley engines were built for speed and the Stanier locos for both speed and hauling power. Andre Chapelon in particular was a magical engineer and innovator who both converted existing designs and produced new Pacifics to suit the operating conditions in France. However I consider that the number one position must go to the German 012 Pacifics because of the way they were developed and what they achieved. At the end of their lives, albeit oil fired they were still working express trains on diesel timings. I will never forget standing at the north end of the platform at Rheine station in north Germany and watching 012 066 seemingly dormant, but then suddenly alive after the fireman had turned on the fuel and made the engine ready for the road in a few minutes. It then took a heavy train non-stop to Leer in well under even time. In Germany they were considered to be equal to diesels!

They had a fairly long and interesting history. In April 1920 a central engineering management was set up in

TABLE ONE

	Rebuilt Merchant Navy	Duchess	DB 012
Weight in Working Order	97.9 tons	106.4 tons	111.6 tons
Driving Wheel Diameter	6ft 2ins	6ft 9ins	6ft 7ins
Cylinders	3	4	3
	18ins x 24ins	16½ins x 28ins	19⅝ins x 26ins
Total Heating Surface	2,451 sq ft	2,807 sq ft	2,221 sq ft
Steam Pressure	250 lb sq ins	250 lb sq ins	227 lb sq ins

Berlin in order to design and implement new standard designs for the unified Reichsbahn. The chief engineer was R.P. Wagner who was a very practical person, inheriting the traditions of the Prussian State Railways. He set about not only producing the new standard designs which could work under all conditions and anywhere in this geographically diverse country, but also a new numbering system which took in the more than 250 different classes inherited from the old companies and which also allowed the new standard classes to be included. There were to be twenty-nine new standard classes including in 1925 the 2-cylinder 01 Pacifics with a working pressure of 227 lb/sq in, 6′ 6¾″ driving wheels and a maximum speed of 130kph/81mph with an axle load of 20.4 tonnes/20 tons. Commercial pressures to reduce journey times between main centres such as Berlin and Hamburg led to the introduction of the diesel unit *Flying Hamburger* but this did not have the capacity needed on this or other routes and so a solution was sought by developing the existing Pacific designs, firstly with an enlarged 01 with 7′ 6½″ driving wheels, 284lb/sq in boiler pressure and a maximum speed of 175kph/110mph. On trial, one of these engines reached 124mph in 1934. These locomotives were 4-6-4s and were still not really designed to haul heavy trains, sometimes on steeply graded main lines throughout Germany. So in 1939 another modified version of the 01 was produced, with three cylinders, improved valve and cylinder design and a top speed of 150kph/94mph. Fifty-five engines were built before the outbreak of the Second World War, the first few being streamlined, although this was subsequently removed. They were classified 01_{10}, later to become 012.

Table 1 sets out the dimensions of the 01_{10} Pacifics and for comparison those of the Merchant Navy and Duchess locomotives. Both of the latter of course were coal fired and although initially coal fired the 3-cylinder 01s were converted to oil firing in 1951. Other improvements were also made at this time including new boilers, relocated sandboxes, small smoke deflectors instead of the standard full sized variety, and roller bearings.

It can be seen from the table that the heating surface of the 01 was comparatively modest compared to the large boilers. This was the form in which the 012 Pacifics as they were to become bore the brunt of front line express work in Germany, shared with the 3-cylinder 03 Pacifics, hauling trains of up to 600 tonnes/590 tons on near mile-a-minute timings until electrification began to displace them. For instance in the mid 1950s there were about ninety daily steam hauled expresses over the busy Rhine valley route between Köln and Mainz, over thirty of which were booked at better than even time, despite an overall speed limit of 120kph/75mph. In the last few years, even the remaining work was of course significant, involving heavy expresses between Osnabruck and Hamburg, Eilzugs (semi-fast trains) and summer relief trains between Rheine and Norddeich and cover for diesels on very fast timings albeit with relatively light loads in the Hamburg and Rheine areas.

I will now look at a few examples of locomotive performance towards the end of the lives of these engines. I didn't start going to West Germany until 1971

11 November 1972. 012.084 storms through the pine woods near Lathen with the 10.54 Norddeich to Rheine.

by which time the areas of operation of the 012 Pacifics were confined to the Hamburg to Westerland, Kiel and Flensburg routes and to the Rheine to Emden line. All of these routes are relatively easily graded, so timings on the trains to which the higher speed limits applied were tight, with a number of mile-a-minute bookings. Some trains were subject to an overall 110kph/70mph, or some Eilzugs as low as 100kph/62mph speed limit so train timing could be a rather dreary process (not so with hindsight!). Apart from these however the general line limit in the Hamburg area was 140kph/87mph and 120kph/75mph in the Rheine area, speeds which were reached and often, towards the end at Rheine, exceeded on a daily basis.

Determined running was necessary in order to keep time on some trains. For instance the 13.50 Rheine to Emden had an overall booking of 101 minutes for 87.80 miles, with 6 intermediate stops, and included 2 sections requiring mile-a-minute start to stop running, one over as little as 12.60 miles. On 13 February 1971 012 052 on the normal light load of 4 cars for 115 tons ran the 19.25 miles from Rheine to Lingen in 18 minutes 45 seconds with a maximum of only 73mph. Later in the run the 3.30 miles from Aschendorf to

11 September 1973. 012.077 on the 17.32 Rheine to Norddeich near Bentlage.

Papenburg took only 4 minutes 16 seconds start to stop with an explosive start reaching 60mph in only 1 minute 49 seconds and 70 in an incredible 2 minutes 23 seconds. Overall time was kept on this run, despite a signal stop before Lathen, probably because the crossing barriers were not lowered in time. Perhaps the signalman was visiting the well known Hotel Bruns, where up trains could be photographed from Room 9 and excellent German food and beer were accompanied by pre war German marching music on 78 rpm records. What a pity that the owner's ambition to preserve an 012 on the hotel forecourt came to nothing. Lathen is also where I obtained one of my best ever tape recordings in April 1975. On a very wet evening 012 063 on the 20.52 ex Rheine departed into the night full blast without a trace of slipping and could be heard for a long time before its exhaust noise was finally lost in the pouring rain. More of this line later in the article.

16 April 1975. Hotel Bruns at Lathen.

A visit to Hamburg in April 1971 resulted in recording some excellent running on a variety of mainly tightly timed trains. After catching the afternoon Dover to Ostend ferry and travelling overnight from Ostend to Hamburg, we caught the 05.38 from Hamburg Altona to Neumünster behind 012 104, the objective being to sample the running on the very

11 July 1974. 012.082 at Rheine with the 13.35 to Norddeich.

fast 06.44 Kiel to Hamburg, which on this day was formed of 7 cars of 258 tonnes tare or about 275 tons gross, hauled by 012 001. The performance was superb, with the engine being thrashed away from each stop into high speed. The overall booking of 48 minutes for the 46.35 miles from Neumünster to Hamburg with two intermediate stops required running of the highest order to keep time, and so it proved on this day. The 13.75 miles from Neumünster to Wrist were run in 12 minutes 45 seconds start to stop, an average of 64.70mph, with a maximum speed of 87mph accompanied throughout by a continuous roar from the engine. This was followed by 12 minutes 50 seconds for the 13.40 miles from Wrist to Elmshorn, with a maximum of 83½mph and a slight easing to observe the speed restriction at Horst. The running on to Hamburg was also fine but slightly spoilt by checks. Overall time was only just kept despite the very high quality performance

TABLE TWO – 0644 KIEL TO HAMBURG

Date	24 April 1971
Train	0644 Kiel to Hamburg
Engine	012 4-6-2 No 012.001
Load	7 coaches, 258 tonnes tare, 275 tons gross
Weather	dry, cold and calm

	miles	sched	mins	secs	speed
Neumünster	0.00	0.00	00	00	
Block Padenstadt	2.30		03	42	70
Arpsdorf	5.60		06	07	83
Brockstedt	8.70		08	18	87
Quarnstedt	11.25		10	05	86½
Wrist	13.75	13.00	12	45	
	0.00	0.00	00	00	
Block Sieb	2.85		03	58	71
Dauendorf	6.15		06	34	82
KM Post 39	8.25		08	09	83½
Horst	9.30		08	54	78*
KM Post 33	12.00		10	51	83
Elmshorn	13.40	0013	12	50	
	0.00	0000	00	00	
KM Post 26	2.85		04	28	67
Tornesch	4.65		05	59	76
Prisdorf	7.10		07	44	80
Pinneberg	9.20		09	51	tsr *53
Halstenbeck	11.50		12	05	68/70½
Edelstedt	15.25		15	21	*60/sigs*
Hamburg Altona	19.20	20.00	21	40	

net time 18¾ minutes
start to stop average Neumünster to Wrist 64.70mph
start to stop average Wrist to Elsmshorn 62.67mph

11 July 1974. 012.080 at Salzbergen on the 13.35 Norddeich to Koln.

11 July 1974. 012.082 waits at Rheine with the 13.35 to Norddeich.

12 July 1974. 012.063 near Meppen on the 13.35 Rheine to Norddeich.

with speeds up to the line limit. The full log of this run is in Table 2.

The day continued with a run round to Hamburg Hbf behind East German Pacific 01 0503 on the 08.03 corridorzug to Berlin, before returning to Altona to catch the 10.09 to Niebull on the Westerland line behind 012 084 hauling 265 tons gross. Some 3 minutes of an 18 minute late start were regained en route with some fairly good running up to 75mph, but also long sections in the early 60s, presumably because of the line limit. We returned to Husum behind 012 073 for an excellent late lunch in the station Gaststätte before travelling across country to Flensburg, firstly in a four-wheeled railbus and then a diesel unit. The objective for our last run of the day was the 17.30 Flensburg to Hamburg D330.

'Nord Pfeil' express originated from Frederikshavn in northern Denmark at 11.40, with a ferry connection from Sweden. This train had moderately fast timings due to its fairly heavy load. We had 012 104 on 8 cars and 3 vans, a total of about 415 tons gross. Departure was nearly 16 minutes late and some fine running saw 11 minutes regained to Hamburg, the only out of course delay being a relaying restriction near Pinneberg. Running was generally in the mid to upper 70s with a maximum of 79mph. The 30.55 miles from km post 67 to km post 18 were run in 24 minutes 18 seconds at an average speed of 75.43mph and the 49.30 miles from Neumunster to Hamburg Hbf ran in 48 minutes 50 seconds, the last section being heavily restricted. Overall the 111.85 miles from Flensburg to Hamburg were covered in 123 minutes 17 seconds despite three intermediate stops, an excellent performance on a cold snowy evening.

So now back to the delights of Rheine. I recorded so many consistently good 012 performances on the line to Emden that it is difficult to pick the best. However a visit in July 1974 produced some high quality running and some good photo opportunities. The line from Rheine to Norddeich is easily graded and slightly downhill overall. There is a climb at about 1 in 280 from Meppen to km post 274 then a roughly equal descent to the aforementioned Lathen, of Bruns fame. The main impediments to high speed progress on this line, apart from the

012 055-0

individual speed restrictions placed on certain trains, were the line limits caused mainly by the four single line sections and also by the state of the track, the latter being improved gradually over the period from 1971 to 1974. Photographically, this line is fairly boring, unless you like flat open landscapes, pine forests, sand dunes and heathlands, crossed occasionally by canals. It could be cold and forbidding as it was on our visit in January 1972, when the maximum temperature was –6°C and the canals were frozen and covered with chunks of ice. Norddeich was the terminus for holidaymakers heading for the coast of Ostfriesland and this was catered for by summer extra trains from all parts of Germany for those hardy enough to brave the cold winds of this area. These trains were normally 012 hauled in the 1970s and often produced good performances, as the accompanying logs show. All permanent speed restrictions, including the single line sections, are shown with an asterisk. The 120kph/75mph speed limit was treated with some disdain towards the end of express steam in West Germany, as were similar limits in England. Who remembers that there was an 85mph limit on the Southern, when Nine Elms drivers were often getting 90 or even 100mph from their steeds? I don't know if the same 'pay by results' culture existed at Rheine, but certainly the engine crews were inspired by the many enthusiasts who came from all over the world to pay homage to the end of Western European express steam power. So, as we have seen, although the route is easy, full speed could not be maintained throughout for various reasons and the 012s had to be worked fairly hard to keep to schedule.

The 11 July 1974 saw us at Rheine after an early morning crossing from Dover to Ostend and an uncomfortable ride on an EMU from Ostend to Bruxelles, followed by three EL hauled trains to our initial destination. My notes confirm that the Hotel Freye in Rheine cost only 20DM for Bed and Breakfast (£6.45 in today's money), and it was clean and tidy as well! After booking in we returned to the station for a short trip to Salzbergen on the 13.52 train with 012 055 to spend the afternoon photographing 012s and various freight locos which appeared at frequent intervals in the fine weather. An evening trip to Lingen with 012 080 out and 012 055 back concluded the day's proceedings.

The next day produced a reasonable run on D1337, the 09.12 Rheine to Norddeich summer relief train with 012 066, just keeping the 68 minute schedule for the 71.05 miles to Leer with 360 tons gross and a maximum speed of 77½mph. This was followed by a very good run on the 10.20 from Leer (09.20 from Norddeich) D715 express

OPPOSITE: 12 July 1974. 012.055 on the 15.09 Norddeich to Rheine, south of Meppen.

TABLE THREE – 0920 NORDDEICH

Date	12 July 1974
Train	0920 Norddeich to München
Engine	012 Class 4-6-2 No. 012.081
Load	7 coaches, 271 tonnes tare, 285 tons gross
Weather	cloudy and warm

	miles	sched	mins	secs	speed
Leer	0.00	0.00	00	00	
KM Post 320	2.00		03	36	58½
Irhove	4.90	6.00	06	01	72
Steenfelde	6.80		07	36	76
KM Post 310	8.20		08	42	79
Papenburg	10.60	11.00	10	50	*51
Aschendorf	13.90	14.00	14	06	72½
KM Post 296	16.90		16	40	*57
Dorpen	19.75	19.00	19	08	68
Kluse	22.50	22.00	21	26	74
KM Post 284	24.25		23	08	70
Lathen	27.40	26.00	25	41	74
KM Post 274	30.60		28	22	68½
Haren	32.80	30.00	30	09	73
Hemsen	36.20	33.00	32	56	76
Meppen	39.20	36.00	35	36	*62
Geeste	46.10	43.00	41	33	75½
Holthausen	48.75	46.00	43	48	76
Lingen	51.75	48.30	46	14	66
Elbergen	56.70		52	10	tsr *44
Leschede	60.65		55	49	75
KM Post 221	63.50		57	52	80
Salzbergen	66.20	61.00	60	04	*61
KM Post 212	69.10		62	46	67½
Block Bentlage	69.70		63	20	*51
Rheine	71.05	66.00	65	17	

net time 63 minutes
*brakes or speed restriction
start to stop average 65.3mph

to München. This train had a very tight timing of 66 minutes for the 71.05 miles to Rheine. On this day 012 081 with 7 cars, 285 tons gross beat this with a time of 65 minutes 17 seconds including a long but moderate permanent way restriction north of Elbergen. Maximum speed was 80mph and net time 63 minutes. Actual start to stop average was 65.3mph. The full log is shown in Table 3.These two runs produced my only ever back-to-back mile-a-minute steam runs anywhere. From leaving Rheine to arriving back there, 142.10 miles occupied only 135 minutes 24 seconds involving a fairly rapid transfer from one side of Leer station to the other in less than two minutes. Further photoing and a return from Meppen to Rheine with 012 082 on the 19.28 train concluded the day's proceedings.

The next day we again travelled on D1337, the 09.12 Rheine to Norddeich as far as Emden. This was headed by an immaculate 012 066 hauling 10 cars totalling 410 tons, including sleepers which originated in Austria. The running, shown in Table 4, was superb, with excesses not justified by the timetable, but probably inspired by the group of Eisenbahnfreunde in the front coach. Note the slow start, the nearly 10mph excess of the speed limit at Meppen, the 82mph maximum speed at Lathen, and the bone shaking rush through Papenburg, again 10mph over the speed limit. The overall time of 63 minutes 47 seconds for the 71.05 miles, or just over 62 minutes net at an actual average of 66.9mph was quite brilliant. The continuation to Emden was spoilt by signal checks, which could sometimes be a problem on this section. Most of the rest of the day was spent visiting Emden shed, where twenty-nine locos in steam were noted, nearly all 2-10-0 heavy freight, although no 012s were present. This was followed by three average to good runs with 012s 066, 080 and 100 and a return to the white cliffs via the 00.48 from Munster and the 10.15 Ostend on the good ship *Königen Elizabeth.*

My final trip of many to Rheine was in April 1975 which was planned as a final farewell to the 012 Pacifics as well as a last look at one of the steam operated rural lines in the Rhine valley area. I arrived at Rheine in good time to catch D714, the 07.07 München to Norddeich due to depart Rheine at 16.50 on tight timings to Emden. 012 075 was in charge of 6 cars total 230 tons gross. This was, as usual, a very good run and the section from Meppen to Leer is shown in Table 5. The 28.60 miles were completed in 27 minutes 37 seconds, a gain of 1 minute on schedule, despite a permanent way restriction approaching Papenburg, giving a net time of just under 27 minutes, with no real effort shown. The 10.60 miles on to Leer were booked in only 11 minutes, a diesel timing which was not kept very

TABLE FOUR – 0912 RHEINE

Date	13 July 1974
Train	0912 Rheine to Norddeich
Engine	012 Class 4-6-2 No 012.066
Load	12 coaches, 385 tones tare, 410 tons gross
Weather	rain

	miles	sched	mins	secs	speed
Rheine	0.00	0.00	00	00	
Block Bentlage	1.35		03	20	44
Salzbergen	4.85	6.00	07	11	64
Leschede	10.40	10.00	11	54	75½
Elbergen	14.35	13.00	15	12	*66
Lingen	19.30	19.00	19	26	74/72
Holthausen	22.30	22.30	22	54	75½
Geeste	24.95	24.00	24	02	76
Meppen	31.95	30.00	29	43	*68½
Hemsen	34.85	33.00	32	38	sigs *47
Haren	38.25	36.00	36	04	68
KM Post 274	40.45		37	56	72
Lathen	43.65	41.00	40	26	82
KM Post 284	46.70		42	45	77½/79
Kluse	48.55	45.00	44	19	75
Dorpen	51.30	47.00	46	32	*65
Aschendorf	57.15	52.00	51	29	74½
Papenburg	60.45	58.00	54	14	*70
Steenfelde	64.25	61.00	57	29	73
Irhove	66.15	63.00	58	59	75
Leer	71.05	68.00	63	47	

net time 62¼ minutes
*brakes or speed restriction
start to stop average 66.9mph

12 July 1974. 012.055 leaving Meppen on the 15.09 Norddeich to Köln.

12 July 1974. 012.066 waiting to take over the 09.12 to Norddeich.

21 March 1975. 012.075 near Haren on the 09.20 Norddeich to München.

TABLE FIVE – MEPPEN TO LEER

Date	15 April 1975				
Train	0707 München to Norddech				
Engine	012 Class 4-6-2 No. 012.075				
Load	6 coaches, 221 tonnes tare, 230 tons gross				
Weather	rain				
	miles	sched	mins	secs	speed
Meppen	0.00	00.00	00	00	
Hemsen	3.00		04	24	60
Haren	6.40		07	29	70½
KM Post 274	8.60		09	21	68½
Lathen	11.80		11	54	76
KM Post 282	13.60		13	20	73/75
Kluse	16.70		16	05	71
Dorpen	19.45		18	25	*60
Aschendorf	25.30		23	45	70½
KM Post 304	27.25		25	49	tsr *48/55
Papenburg	28.60	28.30	27	37	
	0.00	0.00	00	00	
Steenfelde	3.80		04	58	67
Irhove	5.70		06	35	74
KM Post 318	7.35		07	49	75
Leer	10.60	11.00	11	10	
	*brakes or speed restriction				

often. However our reliable beast, at the very end of its life, managed it in only 11 minutes and 10 seconds with a maximum of 75mph. It was at this speed at km post 318 in heavy rain that I passed a personal milestone of 100,000 miles behind steam, an emotional moment that could only have been surpassed if haulage had been with a Bulleid Pacific. And so a quiet run back to Lathen behind 012 081 followed by an excellent meal at The Bruns and the superb tape recording mentioned earlier ended many thousands of miles of thrash behind the magnificent 012 Pacifics.

2 March 1975.
An 012 near Kluse on the 17.40 Rheine to Emden.

21 March 1975. 012.055 storms south near Haren with the 07.53 Norddeich to Köln.

Chapter Nineteen

Seaton Branch – Then and Now

24 July 1962. 30125 near Colyford with the 6.10 pm Seaton to Seaton Junction.

"It was a good line for photography with barely a mile of level track and lovely scenery throughout"

14 April 2014. Car 6 (1954) waits to leave Colyton for Seaton.

On 14 April 2014 we visited the Seaton Tramway for the first time and while we waited at Colyton for our tram to arrive, I reflected on the last time I had been to this line, over fifty years ago in July 1962. This chapter is a photographic essay comparing now with then. With two friends, we were on a Southern Rail Rover, intent on covering as many Southern branch lines as possible, and had arrived at Seaton Junction in the afternoon of 24 July, having travelled from our overnight camping stop near Halwill Junction via Wadebridge, Exeter, Exmouth and Sidmouth, all with steam haulage of course. Waiting for us was M7 0-4-4 tank 30125 which took us to Seaton on the 3.25 pm departure, after we had alighted from the 2.49 pm from Sidmouth Junction, hauled by rebuilt Merchant Navy class 4-6-2 35006. We then backtracked to Colyford, where we found a suitable place to camp overnight in a field next to the line. So of course we spent the rather cloudy evening photographing 30125 coming and going on its 2-coach push-pull set, plus BR class 3 2-6-2 tank 82010 on a light freight train. The following morning was bright and sunny so we lingered for a while taking more shots of 30125, after we had travelled behind it double-headed

25 July 1962. 82010 near Colyford with a freight to Seaton.

with 82010 on the first train of the day to Seaton Junction. 30125 even worked a mixed train into Seaton Junction before we finally left behind rebuilt Battle of Britain class Pacific 34059.

The 4¼ mile line from Seaton Junction to Seaton via Colyton and Colyford was opened in 1868 and closed in March 1966. The line was converted to a tramway between 1969 and 1971 by Claude Lane, who had bought the line. He had previously operated trams in Eastbourne as a visitor attraction. The 2¾ mile route runs between the coastal resort of Seaton and Colyton via Colyford, where we had camped that night. The track gauge is 2ft 9ins and the tramcars are powered by a 132 volt direct current overhead line system. This is very unusual, if not unique, as the supply is actually from banks of batteries located at three locations and fed from the National Grid via solid state converters. Thirteen tram cars are operated, all half-scale replicas of classic British tram cars from various cities. One of them, No 19, is the only tram from the Exeter system which is still in existence. A number of the tramcars are from the closed Eastbourne operation. Some of the lineside infrastructure from the days as a standard gauge branch line can still be seen, such as the concrete hut at Colyford seen in one of the photographs, which now houses electrical supply equipment. In 2014 we rode this tramway on a beautiful sunny spring day, to the relocated terminus in Seaton, the best section being the last mile or so along the Axe estuary. I even spotted the field next to the line where we had camped all those years ago. A ride on this lovely tramway is not to be missed.

25 July 1962. 30125 leaving Seaton Junction with the 8.49 am to Seaton.

24 July 1962. 30125 on the 5.09 pm Seaton to Seaton Junction near Colyford.

14 April 2014. Car 10 (2006 in Glasgow livery) arrives at Seaton from Colyton.

14 April 2014. Car 11 dating from 2007 arrives at Colyton from Seaton. The old line to Seaton Junction used to continue from here.

25 July 1962. 82010 and 30125 arriving at Colyford on the 7.50 am Seaton to Seaton Junction.

25 July 1962. 30125 at Seaton Junction on the 8.10 am to Seaton.

14 April 2014. Car 10 (2006) leaving Colyton for Seaton.

14 April 2014. Colyton station sign.

24 July 1962. 30125 on the 7.41 pm Seaton to Seaton Junction near Colyford.

25 July 1962, Seaton Junction. 82010 and 30125 on the 7.50 am from Seaton.

14 April 2014.The remains of Seaton Junction station.

14 April 2014. Car 6 (1954) approaching Tye Lane Loop on its way to Colyton.

Chapter Twenty

Hayling Seaside Railway

Hayling Seaside Railway, 21 April 2013. *Wendy* and No 1 climb away from the coast at Beachlands with the 11.45 train.

"Re-christened as 'The Hayling Seaside Railway' it has gone from strength to strength each successive year"

Hayling Seaside Railway 21 April 2013. *Wendy* with No 3 and No 5 at Beachlands.

On Sunday, 21 April 2013 the Hayling Seaside Railway's trains were steam worked, a rare occurrence, the last occasion being in September 2010. The engine concerned was Bagnall 2091, a 0-4-0ST built in 1919 for use on the Dorothea Colliery in North Wales and named *Wendy*. It is usually kept at Bursledon Brickworks and was moved to Beachlands on Tuesday, 16 April. It worked all trains with Diesel Loco Number 1, Allan B, provided as train engine for braking power, and made a fine sight in the spring sunshine on this 2-foot gauge seaside railway, which is now threatened with closure.

The one-mile long Hayling Seaside Railway began life as the East Hayling Light Railway, formed by Bob Haddock, a member of the ill fated group who in the mid 1980s attempted to re-instate the 'Hayling Billy' Line. Havant Borough Council had already decided to turn the disused railway line into a cycleway & footpath which precluded any chance of rebuilding the line as standard gauge. Bob with some other like minded members suggested a narrow gauge railway, but that was dismissed by the society committee who declared that it had to be standard gauge or nothing. Sadly at the end of the day that was what they got – nothing. Bob, along with a number of other avid

Hayling Seaside Railway, 21 April 2013. No 1 Allan B at Beachlands.

Hayling Seaside Railway, 21 April 2013. *Wendy* and No 1 pass Mengham Halt with the 12.05 from Eastoke.

Hayling Seaside Railway, 21 April 2013. 0-4-0ST *Wendy* at Beachlands prior to working the 11.45 train.

21 April 2013. Bursledon-based *Wendy* at Beachlands.

fans, decided to set about creating their own railway elsewhere on Hayling Island. After numerous setbacks – all the chosen sites were refused planning permission by the council – eventually a site was found within the Mill Rythe Holiday Camp. So the EHLR was born and ran successfully for many years. Perhaps inspired by the success of the EHLR, Havant Council took the unexpected step of including a railway in their draft plan for Hayling's popular Pleasure Beach. Bob jumped at the idea of running the railway at a more lucrative and prestigious location and submitted a plan for a narrow gauge railway to meet the Council's criteria. Despite many problems and objections to the plan, and after a campaign lasting over twelve years, permission to build the railway was granted. Following closure of the EHLR at Mill Rythe, work started in October 2001 on the building of Beachlands Station on land leased from the neighbouring Funland Amusement Park. Red tape held up the track laying until May 2002. Work continued through 2002 and into 2003 although the original target of opening at Easter 2003 was not met. The line finally opened to passengers on 5 July 2003, running just under a mile to Eastoke with one intermediate halt at Mengham Road just under half way from Beachlands. Re-christened as 'The Hayling Seaside Railway' it has gone from strength to strength each successive year. Now however the owners of Funland Amusement Park want to redevelop the area; there are no plans to retain the station at Beachlands and the railway's terminus is to be relocated.

Hayling Seaside Railway, 21 April 2013. Cab of 0-4-0ST *Wendy* at Beachlands.

Chapter Twenty-One

Hammersmith 150

Hammersmith 150 on 9 August 2014. Met No 1 passes Shepherds Bush Market with the 13.13 Hammersmith to Moorgate.

"The reaction of ordinary members of the public was a joy to watch"

Hammersmith 150 on 9 August 2014. No 12 *Sarah Siddons* heads the 09.55 from Moorgate at Goldhawk Road.

Following the huge success of the Underground steam event of January 2013, London Transport Museum decided to follow this up with a double celebration in August 2014. First on two consecutive weekends was Hammersmith 150, which as its name implies was an event to commemorate the 150th anniversary of the opening of the Hammersmith and City underground line, and then a week later another event with steam on the Chesham branch.

Trains for the Hammersmith event were made up of Metropolitan Locomotive No 1, Metropolitan Milk Van, the Chesham Set, the beautifully restored Jubilee Coach 353 and the 1920s Sarah Siddons electric locomotive No 12. There were five journeys in all, the first hauled by No 1 from Northfields to Moorgate, then three return trips Moorgate to Hammersmith Sarah Siddons hauled out and steam hauled back and finally a return journey back to Northfields, hauled by the electric loco. Prices for a journey varied from £40 to £95 depending on the choice of carriage, the majority paying £60 for a ride in the Bluebell's Chesham set.

We decided to photograph the Hammersmith event and buy tickets to travel on two of the Chesham event trains and so found ourselves on the District line from Victoria to Hammersmith on Saturday, 9 August after an uneventful journey to London via Southern, a rarity nowadays. Arrival across the road at the Hammersmith and City (H&C) line terminus saw quite a crowd gathered and news that the 09.55 from Moorgate was running about twenty minutes late

Hammersmith 150 on 9 August 2014. Met No 1 stands at platform 4 at Moorgate after arrival with the 10.58 from Hammersmith.

9 August 2014. Met No 1 at Moorgate after arrival with the 10.58 from Hammersmith.

due to signalling problems at Aldgate having disrupted the H&C line services, so we jumped on a train to Goldhawk Road in good time to get the first shots of the day, waiting there for the 10.58 from Hammersmith as there was no certainty that a clear view would be possible at Hammersmith as the heritage train would be occupying Platform 1 and H&C trains probably Platform 2. Met No 1 looked and sounded great storming past Goldhawk Road in the sun. That engine certainly raises the echoes when worked hard.

As we wanted some shots at the other end of the line we then caught an H&C train to Moorgate which got us there eventually after a very slow journey, during which its destination was changed after being held for quite a while at Edgware Road, no doubt as a result of earlier problems. Photography at Moorgate wasn't easy as flash was prohibited and I hadn't brought a tripod so it was a case of very high ISO and hold your breath, literally! Fortunately my Canon has a reputation for producing good results even in poor light using a high ISO number. We had intended to get a shot of the 12.10 departure at Barbican, but an eastbound H&C service had other ideas, blocking our view, so all the way back to Hammersmith where our train used Platform 3 allowing a quick window of opportunity to grab some shots of No 1 before another H&C arrival blocked the view by occupying Platform 2. Finally to Shepherds Bush Market for more photos before returning home.

Hammersmith 150 on 9 August 2014. No 12 *Sarah Siddons* on the rear of the 13.13 from Hammersmith approaching Wood Lane BBC.

Hammersmith 150 on 9 August 2014. Met No 1 at Goldhawk Road on the rear of the 09.55 from Moorgate.

Hammersmith 150 on 9 August 2014. Met No 1 storms past Goldhawk Road with the 10.58 Hammersmith to Moorgate.

Hammersmith 150 on 9 August 2014. Met No 1 stands at Hammersmith with the 13.13 to Moorgate.

I found the whole event quite amazing really and yet so normal in many ways. After all, the engines and stock belong on the Underground don't they? The reaction of ordinary members of the public was a joy to watch and I was asked by a number of foreign tourists, American and French, for the times of later steam trains. The action by the Fire Brigade Union fortunately did not affect proceedings – a lot of the line is anyway underground and the rest mainly through chimney pots. London Underground and TfL are to be congratulated on their realistic and enlightened attitude in allowing such events, in contrast to those who run the big railway who throw in the towel at the slightest hint of anything which might affect their key performance indicators, the bonus culture and of course risk aversion. Wooden stock, a steam engine working hard and an ancient electric loco: sheer anathema to the big railway, but fine on LU lines. Well done to them. I do wonder though about the pricing. On the 12.10 train from Moorgate there were many empty seats. Maybe it was just a bit too expensive for the second time around? Great stuff though for 2014.

Hammersmith 150 on 9 August 2014. No 12 *Sarah Siddons* stands at Moorgate on the 12.10 to Hammersmith.

Chapter Twenty-Two

On the Footplate

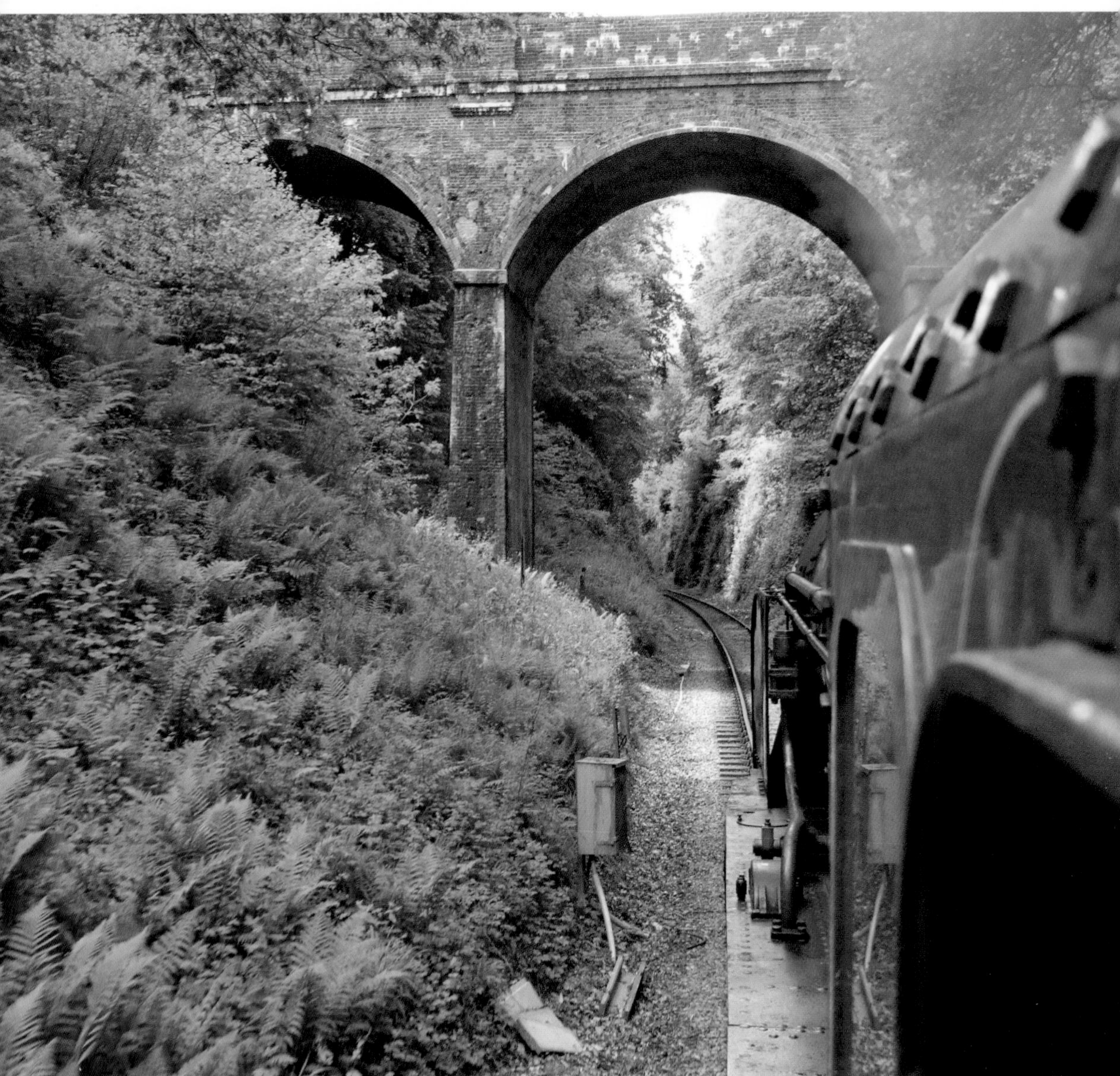

30 May 2015. Climbing to Medstead on 850.

"There is something magic about being on the footplate of a steam engine working hard at speed on the main line"

LEFT: Drivers side of 850 *Lord Nelson* on 30 May 2015.

RIGHT: A good fire on 850, 30 May 2015.

There is something magic about being on the footplate of a steam engine working hard at speed on the main line and this chapter looks at some of the many unofficial rides I had in the days of steam, plus a recent one on the Mid-Hants Railway, given to me as a birthday present by my wife. Inevitably my trips were all on the Southern (except for one brief episode on a DR Class 86 tank) and as it happens all on Bulleid pacifics. The first came during the course of a Southern Rail Rover in April 1964. I had settled into a routine of going down to Salisbury on the 11 am from Waterloo, the Atlantic Coast Express (ACE), returning on the 2.09 pm up ACE, going down to Southampton on the 4.35 pm Royal Wessex and then back up on the 7.16 pm fast, though I did ring the changes to get some variety. At that time a Weymouth crew brought the 7.16 pm up as far as Southampton, where Eastleigh enginemen took over. Whilst waiting on the platform that Monday evening I got chatting to the driver, who told me his name was Roy Sloper and so began a firm friendship which lasted until the end of steam and beyond with occasional meetings; at the time of writing he is still around, now in his nineties. Our engine that day was No 35029 *Ellerman Lines* and with the usual load of ten coaches and a van totalling around 385 tons we left three and a half minutes late and with a clear run ran into Waterloo two minutes early. Speed was maintained at 60-61 all the way up Roundwood bank and then in the 70s afterwards but topping 81mph as Roy took full advantage of the clear road through Woking. The time of 78 minutes 28 seconds was nicely inside even time. Roy told me it took very little effort from a free steaming engine and if I was around the next day would I like to see how it was done?

Well of course I would, and so to make quite sure on the Tuesday, 21 April 1964 I changed my routine, returning from Salisbury on the 12.32 pm semi-fast

BELOW: Full cab view of 34028 at Harman's Cross 28 October 2009.

SOUTHHAMPTON TO WATERLOO

Date	21 April 1964
Train	530 pm Weymouth to Waterloo
Engine	Rebuilt Merchant Navy Class 4-6-2 No. 35001 *Channel Packet*
Load	10 coaches and 1 van, 360 tons tare, 390 tons gross
Driver	Roy Sloper, Eastleigh
Position	Footplate

	miles	sched	mins	secs	speed	regulator	cut off %	boiler lb	steam chest lb
Southampton	0.00	0.00	00	00		½		240	150
Northam Junction	1.05	3.30	03	20		closed		230	0
St Denys	2.11		05	09	45	full	30	230	210
Swaythling	3.54		06	54	53	full	25	230	210
Eastleigh	5.80	10.00	09	14	60	full	20	230	210
Allbrook Box	6.66		10	08	62	full	20	230	210
Shawford	9.61		13	12	56	full	15	210	190
Shawford Junction	10.48		14	02	56½	full	15	210	190
St Cross	11.50		15	10	57	full	15	210	190
Winchester City	12.75		16	26	58	full	20	200	180
Winchester Junction	14.85		18	36	63	full	20	180	165
Wallers Ash Box	17.55		21	18	61	full	15	180	160
Weston Box	19.05		22	43	59	full	15	190	170
Micheldever	21.18		24	59	58	full	15	190	170
Roundwood Box	23.05		27	05	56	full	15	180	160
Waltham Box	24.15		28	12	63	½	15	200	120
Steventon Box	25.30		29	20	65	¼	15	215	80
Wootton Box	26.75		30	42	65½	¼	15	230	80
Worting Junction	28.98	37.00	33	02	58*	shut	15	240	0
Basingstoke	31.50		35	18	70½	½	15	230	120
Newnham Siding	35.55		38	36	77	½	15	225	110
Hook	37.08		39	52	72/70	¼	15	220	90
Winchfield	39.41		41	49	73/79	⅓	15	230	120
Fleet	42.76		44	26	76½	½	18	220	140
Farnborough	46.05		47	00	78	½	18	225	140
Sturt Lane Junction	47.05		47	49	74	¼	18	215	110
MP 31	48.25		48	48	70½	¼	15	220	110
Pirbright Junction	49.60		49	56	73	¼	15	215	100
Brookwood	51.25		51	17	75	¼	15	230	90
Woking Junction	54.50	58.00	53	55	72	shut	15	235	0
Woking	54.95		54	18	73	shut	15	230	20
West Byfleet	57.56		56	27	78	½	18	230	150
Byfleet Junction	58.84		57	31	74	⅓	18	230	120
Weybridge	60.09		58	38	69	¼	15	230	110
Oatlands Box	61.15		59	33	67	¼	15	225	110
Walton	62.16		60	26	70	¼	15	225	100
Hersham	63.33		61	21	73	¼	18	225	100
Esher	64.85		62	41	71	shut	18	230	20
Hampton Court Junction	65.90	67.30	63	32	70½	¼	15	225	110
Surbiton	67.20		64	47	67	¼	15	230	110
New Malden	69.46		66	47	72	¼	15	210	100
Wimbledon	72.05		69	06	65				
Earlsfield	73.66		70	45	66				
Clapham Junction	75.31	77.00	72	43	40*				
Queens Road	76.43		74	21	58				
Vauxhall	77.93		76	08	42*				
Waterloo	79.24	84.00	79	11					

start to stop average 60.04mph
depart 1¼ minutes late, arrive Waterloo 3½ minutes early

behind No 34020 *Seaton* so I could go right through to Bournemouth on the 3.30 pm from Waterloo (No 35008 *Orient Line*) and pick up the 7.16 pm from Bournemouth at 6.40 pm with the Weymouth crew as far as Southampton. The engine was No 35001 Channel Packet and the load ten coaches and a van, total about 390 tons. At Southampton I ventured up front wondering if my new friend had remembered his promise. He had, and so soon I was safely ensconced in the fireman's seat for my first ever footplate ride. I can still remember that day very clearly and the overriding impressions of noise, dirt and vibration as we got up to speed. In fact the engine was rough riding for a Bulleid and wasn't steaming very well as the train running log shows. We made a good start and were doing 60mph by Eastleigh nicely inside schedule. Here the driver and fireman both waved at a street near the lineside which was where they lived; they made good use of the whistle. Full regulator was now used until the top of the 1 in 252 climb at Litchfield tunnel and cut off set at 15 per cent. The previous day this had kept speed at a mile a minute but today with pressure dropping speed was about 4 or 5mph lower until Roy increased the cut off to 20 per cent and that together with the slight easing of gradient through Winchester lifted the speed to 63mph before Roy looked at the pressure gauge and decided to ease back to 15 per cent which saw us over the top at 56mph. Bearing in mind that we were only using 160-170 lbs of steam this was an excellent effort and enough to see us past Worting Junction in just over 33 minutes from the start, a gain of four minutes on schedule. From there it was very easy and only needed 15-18 per cent cut off and 110-140 lbs of steam to keep the schedule exactly on to Woking and Clapham Junction with no higher speed than 79mph. It was just as well that the boiler pressure had recovered as the engine wasn't fired after Fleet, not by choice but as a result of the fireman pulling the shovel over the side when he retrieved the pricker from the tender to clean the fire. So with no spare carried the fireman spent the rest of the trip looking for signals and cleaning the footplate. Arrival at Waterloo was nearly four minutes early and I was allowed to alight from the footplate once Roy had ensured the coast was clear of any Inspectors. It was a wonderful experience for this teenager and one that will remain with me always. I had got home to Shirley near Croydon before my hearing returned though!

On the footplate of 850 on 30 May 2015.

On the Wednesday I returned to my usual routine and waiting on the platform at Southampton Roy told me to make sure my stop watch was working properly as that night we were going to attempt something special and I had better be in the train. The train arrived late from Bournemouth and I saw some chat between the Weymouth crew and ours which turned out to be about who would sort out the lost time ticket. Roy said not to worry as we would be on time at Waterloo and so it proved. We had No 35024 *East Asiatic Company* on the usual load, we left 9 minutes late and ran up in under 75 minutes. Speed up the bank was held at 63-65mph and then 76-83mph all the way from Basingstoke to New Malden, averaging 78.9mph between them.

This was my second fastest run ever with steam from Southampton to Waterloo. On Thursday, 23 April we did nearly as well with an ex works 35016 *Elders Fyffes* arriving at Waterloo three minutes early after 63-65mph again up the bank and 85mph near Winchfield after which the engine was eased, but we were

BASINGSTOKE TO WOKING

Date	24 October 1966
Train	350 pm Weymouth to Waterloo
Engine	Rebuilt West Country Class 4-6-2 No. 34034 *Honiton*
Load	11 coaches and 2 vans, 412 tons tare, 445 tons gross
Driver	Roy Sloper, Eastleigh
Position	Footplate

	miles	sched	mins	secs	speed	regulator	cut off %	boiler lb	steam chest lb	
Basingstoke	0.00	0.00	00	00		¼	45	210	80	12 late
MP 46	1.75		03	44	50	¾	30	210	180	local line
Newnham Siding (Site)	4.10		06	07	60	½	20	200	145	
Hook	5.59		08	27	trs *24	shut	35	225	0	
MP 41	6.75		10	26	42	¾	35	195	150	
Winchfield	7.92		12	03	51	full	22	170	160	
MP 38	9.75		13	49	63	½	22	160	100	
Fleet	11.27		15	17	62½	½	22	190	120	
MP 35	12.75		16	48	56½	shut	22	175	0	
Farnborough	14.55		18	35	61	¾	22	205	175	
Sturt Lane	15.60		19	34	62½	¾	22	190	160	
MP 31	16.75		20	44	62	½	30	180	140	
Pirbright Junction	18.26		22	06	67	½	30	170	90	
Brookwood	19.76		24	04	39*	shut	22	180	0	sigs
MP 27	20.75		-	-	45	¼	22	180	30	sigs
Woking Junction	23.00		28	39	23*	shut	50	200	0	sigs
Woking	23.46	28.00	29	56						13 late
	Net time 25 minutes									

running so early that we got a severe signal check at Woking and were checked again at Weybridge and Surbiton. So although our actual time was over 82 minutes the net time was around 74. On the Friday Roy gave me another footplate ride, this time on No 35014 *Nederland Line* and this proved to be the worst run of the week. The engine was very rough riding and steaming badly so needed full regulator and 20 per cent cut off to maintain 53-54mph up the bank. But we were still doing OK to pass Worting Junction a minute early after a two minute late start and, with speed up to 79mph at Fleet, looked set for another early arrival but it was not to be. We got a signal check at Sturt Lane and again at Weybridge but even then Roy tried to get us in on time by running up to a very daring and exhilarating 75mph past Wimbledon where I had to hang on tight as we rounded the curve at the London end. We then sat down outside Waterloo, finally arriving seven minutes late, a poor and untypical end to a fantastic week with a great engineman.

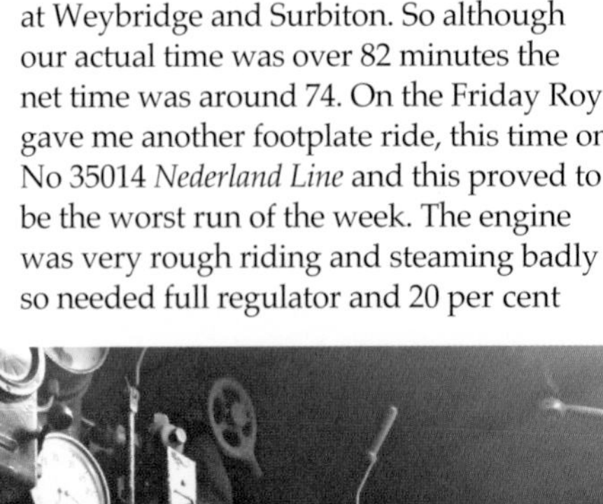

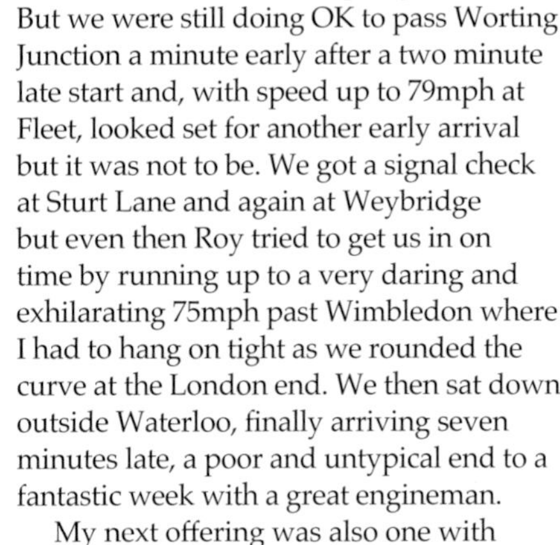

Cab of 70000 *Britannia* working the Royal Duchy on 5 August 2012.

My next offering was also one with Roy Sloper, this time on a heavily loaded up semi-fast train. No 34034 *Honiton* had a load of 13 bogies, just short of 450 tons full and when I climbed up onto the footplate after a warm greeting from Roy it was obvious that all was not well. The boiler pressure was down to 160 lb but had recovered to 210 lb by the time we left, 12 minutes late on the slow line. Roy said that if he tried to use full regulator the pressure

Firing 850 *Lord Nelson* on 30 May 2015.

BASINGSTOKE TO WINCHESTER CITY

Date	13 January 1966
Train	530 pm Waterloo to Weymouth
Loco	Rebuilt West Country Class 4-6-2 No. 34012 *Launceston*
Load	11 coaches, 374 tons tare, 410 tons gross
Driver	Dave Parsons, Nine Elms
Fireman	Harrington, Nine Elms
Weather	Snow
Position	Footplate

	miles	sched	mins	secs	speed	regulator	cut off %	boiler lb	steam chest lb	
Basingstoke	0.00	0.00	00	00		¾	55	240	195	right time
Worting Jct	2.51	5.30	05	52	42	¾	35	230	180	
MP 51	3.20		06	53	47½	full	25	220	210	
Wootton	4.75		08	43	50	full	25	220	210	
Steventon	6.20		13	23	trs *27	shut	20	215	0	
Waltham	7.35		15	51	trs *19	¼	22	240	60	svo
Roundwood	8.45		17	52	47½	½	27	230	190	slipping
Micheldever	10.31		19	55	63	full	20	215	200	
Weston	12.45		21	49	72½	full	15	210	200	
Wallers Ash	13.95		23	01	78	full	15	210	200	
MP 63	15.20		24	02	81	½	15	240	150	svo
Winchester Junction	16.65	21.30	26	58	sigs *12	shut	15	235	0	
MP 65	17.20		27	50	50	½	35	215	90	
Winchester City	18.74	25.00	30	49						

net time 20½ minutes — svo=Safety Valves open

WINCHESTER TO EASTLEIGH

Date	18 February 1966
Train	1035 pm Waterloo to Weymouth
Loco	Rebuilt West Country Class 4-6-2 No. 34037 *Clovelly*
Load	3 coaches and 10 vans, 368 tons tare, 400 tons gross
Driver	Gordon Porter
Fireman	Tom Moult
Weather	Rain
Position	Footplate

	miles	sched	mins	secs	speed	regulator	cut off %	boiler lb	
Winchester	0.00	0.00	00	00		½	70	200	2 mins late
St Cross	1.25		02	45	48½	½	45	170	
Shawford Junction	2.27		03	44	63	full	35	150	
Shawford	3.14		04	38	66	full	35	145	
MP 71	4.50		05	50	69	¼	20	145	
Allbrook Box	6.09		07	42	25*	shut	20	160	
			long	sigs stop	0*	shut	70	190	local line
Eastleigh	6.95	11.00	17	18					
	net time 9 minutes								

FLEET TO WINCHFIELD

Date	5 October 1966
Train	541 pm Waterloo to Salisbury
Loco	Unrebuilt West Country Class 4-6-2 No. 34006 *Bude*
Load	11 coaches, 350 tons tare, 380 tons gross
Driver	Les Cummings
Fireman	Dave Davis
Weather	sunny periods
Position	Footplate

	miles	sched	mins	secs	speed	regulator	cut off %	boiler lb	steam chest lb
Fleet	0.00	0.00	00	00		¼	75	220	60
MP 37	0.52		01	43	25	full	60	220	190
MP 38	1.52		03	20	43½	¾	30	210	170
MP 39	2.52		04	38	49	¾	25	210	170
			trs		33*	shut	25	220	0
Winchfield	3.35	6.30	06						

ALTON TO MEDSTEAD & FOUR MARKS

Date	30 May 2015
Train	1200 Alton to Alresford
Loco	LN Class 4-6-0 No. 850 *Lord Nelson*
Load	5 coaches, 178 tons tare, 200 tons gross
Driver	Phil Hathaway
Fireman	Ollie Collins
Weather	sunny periods
Position	Footplate

	miles	sched	mins	secs	speed	regulator	cut off %	boiler lb	steam chest lb
Alton	0.00	0.00	00	00		½	60	180	80
Butts Junction	1.05		04	57	24/trs*10	½/shut	20	170	110/0
MP 51	1.84		06	53	24	full	30	160	150
MP 52	2.84		09	15	27	full	35	200	190
Hants Hunt Bridge	3.57		11	00	26	full	30	210	200
MP 53	3.84		11	35	26	full	30	210	200
Summit	4.17		12	25	19*	¼	20	200	50
Medstead & Four Marks	4.43	14.00	14	19					

23 August 2006. Driver Tony Leaver at the controls of 75027 entering Horsted Keynes.

would fall rapidly, so he would have to let the engine find its own speed using half regulator. After the slack for track work at Hook, Roy tried full regulator for a while but as predicted this quickly pulled the pressure back to 160 lbs and the boiler needed to be filled, so discretion was the best option and we trundled along with speed in the sixties until the signal checks outside Woking. There I got back into the train and we stood for five minutes while the fireman got the fire into shape and the pressure up to the red line. Things then improved and we reached a nice 75mph at Hersham regaining three minutes to Waterloo. I suspect that the engine was due for a boiler washout and, as I found with other Bulleid Pacifics, when this happens it's no good opening the regulator fully and hoping that will do the trick as it would on an engine in good condition.

The winter and spring of early 1966 was when I had most of my footplate rides. These included some on the 5.30 pm Waterloo to Weymouth with Nine Elms No 4 link driver Dave Parsons, though this train was a No 3 link turn at that time. Even though it was dark, Dave was nervous about letting me ride from Waterloo, so I joined him and fireman Harrington on the footplate at Basingstoke for a ride as far as Winchester. Thursday, 13 January was very cold and snowy but our engine, Rebuilt Pacific No 34012 Launceston, rode smoothly and was steaming well, so only had to be fired lightly. Dave though said it felt sluggish and the 81mph down Roundwood bank after the very long slack for track works from after Wootton to Waltham was poor in comparison with a speed in the nineties obtained with No 34026 the following night with only 150 lbs of steam. My notes say that 34012 was inclined to shake the fire about and towards the front.

Also in the early part of 1966 I had a number of footplate rides with Gordon Porter, another likeable and friendly Nine Elms man who in my opinion was in the top few drivers for producing epic performances from the Bulleid Pacifics in those last few years.

This subject is dealt with fully in my forthcoming book *Southern Steam Twilight: The Untold Story* so I will only dwell briefly here on a snippet from my

30 May 2015. Braking for the stop at Ropley on 850 *Lord Nelson*.

28 October 2009. Drivers side cab view of 34028 *Eddystone*.

favourite driver. I had ridden all the way from Waterloo on No 34037 *Clovelley* working the 10.35 pm down mails and the table shows the final section from Winchester to Eastleigh. Even on this section our fireman, Tom Moult had to work hard but still failed to maintain pressure. The steam chest gauge wasn't working on this engine and no doubt it would have been failed by lesser drivers and of course in the current environment would have failed its fitness-to-run exam on a number of counts. Finally on the main line is a cameo from another of the Nine Elms 'fast men', Les Cummings, whose fireman was Dave Davis, the same man who in the 1990s produced some phenomenal performances with No 35028 *Clan Line*. This was with unrebuilt No 34006 *Bude* on the 5.41 pm Waterloo to Salisbury semi-fast train, which Nine Elms men took as far as Basingstoke. That evening some of the fraternity took it in turns riding from station to station on the Woking to Basingstoke section and it was my turn from Fleet to Winchfield. It

28 October 2009. 34028 *Eddystone* at Harman's Cross.

was nothing special but the engine was completely on top of the job with its 380 ton load. Les was the driver who gave me one of my highest speeds with a Bulleid light Pacific, 97 mph down Roundwood bank and details of this too will be in my next book.

Riding on the footplate on a preserved line with its nominal 25mph speed limit cannot ever be the same as on the main line at high speed, but the run I had in May 2015 with 850 *Lord Nelson* was still a great experience. I was surprised at how relatively hard the engine had to work even taking into account the 1 in 60 climb out of Alton and of just how rough riding it was. This was in part due to my main line experiences all being on Pacifics whereas of course No 850 is a 4-6-0 with no trailing truck to smooth the ride. Maybe I will once again manage a footplate ride with a Bulleid Pacific on the main line but if not the memories of those I had will never fade.

28 October 2009. The hazards of being a footplateman.

Chapter Twenty-Three

Main Line Steam Today

10 December 2009. 34067 *Tangmere* climbs Gomshall bank with the 9.40 am Victoria to Oxford.

"I hope this chapter conveys the impression of what can still be enjoyed by the train timing enthusiast today"

14 July 2011. 70000 *Britannia* passing Willingdon Junction with the empty stock of the 9 am Lewes to Ely.

It is in my view remarkable that today steam hauled trains continue to run on the main line in such numbers. There have been problems of course, the most high profile being the suspension of operator West Coast Railways for some weeks in the Spring of 2015, but still the well filled specials continue often producing locomotive performances of the highest order to equal and in some cases surpassing those achieved in the real days of steam. Some locomotives stand out as being quite exceptional either due to what they are achieving, such as the BR Standard Class 7 Pacific No 70000 *Britannia*, or for their reliability, such as Bulleid Merchant Navy Class Pacific No 35028 *Clan Line*, or for both robustness and performance such as the superb Tyseley Castle Class 4-6-0 No 5043 *Earl of Mount Edgcumbe*. Over the years since the return to steam other engines have also been outstanding and all of this has to be seen within the context of an ever busier railway system and the overall 75mph limit imposed on steam, with many engines restricted to a lower maximum which did not apply in the real days of steam. It would be nice to think that only line speed limits should apply but being realistic we have to remember that all steam engines now working on the main line are old by any measure and must be operated both safely and to minimise wear and tear. Nevertheless some enginemen, even in recent years, have taken the view that if the engine is running well and it feels right then the overall speed limit can take second place to allowing the engine to have its head. I have included two such runs in this chapter, both as it happens on the same

45th ANNIVERSARY SPECIAL, STEAM DREAMS

Date	9 July 2012
Train	1738 Weymouth to Waterloo
Loco	Merchant Navy class 4-6-2 35028 *Clan Line*
Load	11 coaches 392 tons tare, 430 tons gross
Driver	Don Clarke
Fireman	Jim Clarke
Position	11 of 11
Weather	cloudy, damp

	miles	sched	mins	secs	speed
Eastleigh	0.00	0.00	00	00	
Allbrook Box	0.86		02	54	34½/38½
			sigs stop		0*
Shawford	3.81	8.00	14	39	34
Shawford Junction	4.66		15	49	37½
			sigs		33*
St Cross	5.70		17	49	40
Winchester City	6.95	13.00	19	32	48
Winchester Junction	9.05		21	59	56
Wallers Ash Box+	11.75		24	40	59½
Weston Box+	13.25		26	18	61½
Micheldever	15.38		28	19	64½
Roundwood Box+	17.25		30	00	67½
Litchfield Tunnel In	17.60		30	24	68½
Steventon Box+	19.50		31	59	71
Wootton Box+	20.95		33	14	72/74
Battledown	22.45		34	27	72
Worting Junction	23.18	30.00	35	06	75½
Basingstoke	25.70	33.00	37	10	71*
MP 46	27.45		38	35	76/73
Newnham Siding	29.75		40	27	75½/72½
Hook	31.28		41	39	76
Winchfield	33.61		43	34	74
MP 38	35.45		45	00	77
Fleet	36.96		46	13	74/75
Farnborough	40.25	46.00	48	51	74
Sturt Lane Junction	41.25		49	41	72½
MP 31	42.45		50	40	72
Pirbright Junction	43.80		51	45	77
Brookwood	45.45		53	01	75/76½
Woking Junction	48.70	54.00	55	36	75
Woking	49.15	55.00	55	57	76
West Byfleet	51.76		58	03	74½
Byfleet Junction	53.04		59	04	75½
Weybridge	54.29		60	11	71/70
Oatlands Box+	55.35		61	02	72
Walton	56.36		61	51	75½
Hersham	57.55		62	44	75
Esher	59.05		64	02	73½
Hampton Court Jct.	60.10	68.00	64	55	72½
Surbiton	61.40	69.00	65	59	70
New Malden	63.66	71.00	67	51	73½
Raynes Park	64.80		68	48	73
Wimbledon	66.25	73.30	69	57	71½
Earlsfield	67.86		71	30	56*
			sigs		12*
Clapham Junction	69.51	78.00	75	55	35½
			sigs stop		0*
Queens Road	70.63	81.30	83	02	19½
Vauxhall	72.13		85	42	31
			sigs stop		0*
Waterloo	73.44	93.00	92	57	
					* brakes

+ site of box

Weston to Roundwood =1735 edbh, 2300 ihp
Final mile to Litchfield Tunnel = 2,000 edbh, 2600 ihp
67.66 miles from sigs stop before Shawford to sigs stop before Queens Road in 67 mins 53 secs = 59.80mph
Average speed 60.91 miles Winchester to Earlsfield = 70.33mph
Average speed 45.26 miles Wootton to Wimbledon 73.96mph

stretch of railway, but there have been many others elsewhere. Details of the dates and enginemen concerned have of course had to remain anonymous. So here goes with a few recent very good runs with steam that I have been privileged to enjoy in recent years.

Each year on the 9 July, Steam Dreams run a special train to Weymouth to mark the anniversary of the end of Southern steam and each year a group of Southern steam enthusiasts make up a party and enjoy a day out together enjoying the steam haulage and reminiscing over the events of days gone by. One such event was on 9 July 2012 and it was appropriate that Bulleid Merchant Navy Class Pacific No 35028 *Clan Line* was our engine that day. Graeme Bunker, then of Steam Dreams, did us proud by arranging a good path for the up journey back to Waterloo. Although the schedule to Waterloo wasn't very demanding at 93 minutes for the 73½ miles from Eastleigh we had high hopes of a good climb to Roundwood and some fast running afterwards assuming that the path we had been given worked as planned. We knew that first of all a Cross Country service had to pass us and make its Winchester call but that after that we should be clear as far as the London suburbs. I am not sure how many of us actually believed that this would happen but the doubters, myself amongst them, were proved wrong and what followed was the fastest long distance run on Southern metals since 1967.

The accompanying log shows the details but doesn't tell the full story. After the Eastleigh restart we ran up the slow line to stop at the signal just on the country side of milepost 70½ to allow the Voyager to get past, and after we got underway again we were still being impeded with double yellow signals as far as Winchester. But then we got greens, amazingly all the way to Earlsfield, over 60 miles, which we ran at an average speed of over

11 September 2013. 35028 *Clan Line* on the late running 8.45 am Victoria to Bath VSOE passing Wyke, east of Andover.

70mph including getting up to speed after recovery from the checks. There had been talk in our group of a possible 70mph at the top of the 1 in 252 climb to Roundwood and though I was sceptical we actually got very close to this with 68.3mph achieved at the entrance to Litchfield tunnel despite only passing Winchester at 48mph. As we passed the site of Weston Box, speed was just over 60mph but the rate of acceleration was growing which made me think that Don Clarke had increased the cut off or regulator, or both. In fact he had lifted the regulator into the roof and set the cut off at 35 per cent at Winchester and the engine did the rest. So why the rapid rise in speed over the last 4 miles of the climb? Well my old friend from the days of steam, Tony Leaver, a Bluebell Railway driver and one of the group on the train, explained to me afterwards, 'One of the problems with the steam tours is when the loco stops for water, the firebox tends to cool down (more so if the loco has been working fairly hard). From the water stop in the loop before Southampton, the loco would not be working particularly hard to Eastleigh where there was another stop and then a stroll up towards Shawford where there was another stop. So not really time to get the box hot again. When a loco is started (with a good fire) there is often an initial drop in pressure, but this quickly recovers, but this also depends on how hard the loco is being worked, which again relates to the gradients. On this trip the pressure continued to drop to 200 lb until the box and brick arch had warmed up. This might explain the increase in speed after Weston as with an increase in boiler pressure, with full regulator, there would be more pressure in the steam chest.' So it was simply the good old Bulleid syndrome of the boiler pressure increasing the harder the engine was worked. I have calculated the power output during the later stages of the climb and although it didn't set any records it was still excellent at 2,000 equivalent drawbar horsepower and 2,600 indicated horse power for the final mile to Litchfield tunnel.

What followed from Roundwood would not have needed much effort from the engine but was a joy to time and will live long in the memory. When was the last time that a steam train had got a clear road through both Basingstoke and Woking? There is a spine tingling video clip of us passing Woking at full speed on YouTube. And all achieved within the current overall speed limit for steam to give a flying average speed of just under 74mph from Wootton to Wimbledon. It was a superlative effort and a credit to all concerned. So from being nearly 8 minutes late at Winchester we passed Wimbledon 3 minutes early and with lots of time allowed for the finish to Waterloo we realised that signal checks would follow. In fact we very nearly got a second even time run of the day from the signal stop before Shawford to a signal stop before Queens Road despite the adverse signals before Winchester and a severe check before Clapham Junction plus creeping slowly up to the stop: we were just 13 seconds outside the 60mph mark. After another stop we ran into Waterloo just one minute late to stand at the buffer stops just as 35030 had done on the 2.11 pm from Weymouth exactly forty-five years before. It was a fitting that our driver for this wonderful run was Don Clarke, an ex Nine Elms fireman, and that his son Jim was producing the steam for him to work *Clan Line* as he did. I was told afterwards that there was still 3,000 gallons of water left in the tender, so incredibly *Clan Line* had used just 2,700 gallons of water to produce the superb run we had all just witnessed, hardly an excessive amount for a class of engine with a reputation for high water consumption and a tribute to the high standard of maintenance of this engine and to the father and son footplate pair on 9 July.

For my second run I have chosen an outstanding effort from Castle Class 4-6-0 No 5029 *Nunney Castle* which Tyseley had prepared specially for this anniversary special. On 9 May 1964 there took place an Ian Allan special train which commemorated the 60th anniversary of City of Truro's high speed dash down Wellington bank. The superb running that day by all the engines involved (4079, 5054, 7025, 7029 and 6999) will forever be remembered by those who were there and has a permanent place in the history of the steam locomotive. So it was no surprise that two tour companies, Vintage and Pathfinder, decided to run trains to mark the 50th anniversary of 1Z48, the 1964 special, each in a different way. None of the engines used in 1964 could be used, so Vintage opted to use their star performer, 5043 *Earl of Mount Edgcumbe* and Pathfinder 5029 *Nunney Castle*. As I had already had quite a few runs with 5043 and as the Pathfinder tour was on the exact 50th anniversary, plus it involved running both down to Plymouth and back to Bristol, with the final section from Exeter booked in even time, I opted for that trip, 'The Anniversary Ltd', rather than the Vintage Trains 1Z48 on the following day, though both engines carried that famous reporting number 5029 *Nunney Castle* was built at Swindon in 1934. It was initially allocated to Old Oak Common where it spent most of its working life. The engine moved to Worcester in 1958, then had spells at Newton Abbot and Laira before going to Cardiff East Dock in 1962, where it was to remain until being withdrawn in December 1963. *Nunney Castle* was sold to Woodham Brothers at Barry in 1964

The Anniversary Ltd, 9 May 2014. 5029 *Nunney Castle* stands at Westbury prior to taking over the train.

where it was to stay for twelve years. 5029 was in fact the last steam loco delivered to Barry Scrap yard by rail. In 1976 it was sold to a consortium consisting of private individuals and the Great Western Society at Didcot Railway Centre. In the mid 1990s, the private consortium took total control and the loco left Didcot for a life on the main line. It had recently had an intermediate repair at Tyseley, carried out by Bob Meanley and his team. This has seen all of the axleboxes repaired with new bearing steps, horns reground and liners refitted, tyres renewed, journals turned and a piston and valve overhaul. The valves have been reset to determined parameters by the same engineer who set the valves on 5043. It has the original single chimney and two-row low temperature superheater, and therefore performance on the main line, though good and well up to what would be expected of a standard Castle, is not as sparkling as its sister, 5043, which has the benefit of a double chimney and four-row superheater. In practice this difference shows more on the hills than on the level or downhill sections, due to the nominal 75mph speed limit imposed on both engines.

The running all day was excellent but I have chosen to show the log of the non-stop return section from Exeter to Bristol. The HST to Paddington due to go in front of us left slightly late and we got the green signal in time to get us away just over four minutes late. This final section non-stop to Bristol Temple Meads was timed in just 75 minutes for the 75½ miles and I was looking forward to it greatly as the highlight of the day, as it had been back in 1964 when 7029 had run non-stop from Plymouth and, as 5043, would

PATHFINDER TOURS - THE ANNIVERSARY LIMITED

Date	9 May 2014
Train	1634 Plymouth to Bristol Temple Meads
Loco	Castle Class 4-6-0 No 5029 *Nunney Castle*
Load	8 coaches, 290 tons tare, 310 tons gross
Driver	Gareth Jones until after Cogload, then Vince Henderson
Fireman	Vince Henderson until after Cogload, then Dave Proctor
Position	7 of 8
Weather	sunny periods, west wind

	miles	sched	mins	secs	speed
Exeter St Davids	0.00	0.00	00	00	4¼ mins late
Cowley Bridge Junction	1.24	4.00	03	53	36
Stoke Canon	3.70		07	18	48
Silverton	7.13		11	23	54
Hele	8.39		12	45	58
Cullompton	12.56		17	04	62½
MP 180	13.90		18	24	58½/57½
Tiverton Junction	14.74	17.00	19	12	60½/65½
Tiverton Parkway	16.58	19.00	20	53	64½
Burlescombe	19.15		23	24	56½
Whiteball Summit	19.90	23.00	24	12	54½
Beam Bridge	21.88		26	02	73½/78
Wellington	23.70		27	25	76*
Poole Siding	24.90		28	23	73½
Victory Crossing	27.84		30	42	79
Norton Fitzwarren	28.89	31.00	31	31	77/75
Taunton	30.74	33.00	32	58	77½
Creech St Michael	33.65		35	12	79
Cogload Junction	35.50	37.00	36	38	76
MP 155	38.90		39	15	79/76½
Bridgwater	42.32	43.00	41	50	79
MP 148	45.90		44	34	78
Highbridge	48.63		46	43	75
Brent Knoll	51.40		49	00	73
Uphill Junction	55.84	54.00	52	35	75
Worle Junction	58.78	56.00	54	54	77
Worle	59.37		55	22	76
Yatton	63.59		58	42	77
Nailsea	67.45		61	45	73½
Flax Bourton	69.63		63	31	71½
MP 123	70.90		64	36	69
Long Ashton	71.85		65	24	76½/77½
Parson Street	73.73	70.00	66	53	72*
Bedminster	74.58		68	00	34*
Bristol West Junction	75.15	72.00	69	06	25*
Bristol Temple Meads	75.49	75.00	70	22	arr ½ min early

* brakes
average speed 64.37mph start to stop

do the day after our run. Now in charge up front were driver Gareth Jones and fireman Dave Proctor helped by Vince Henderson until he took over driving again somewhere after Cogload, with Traction Inspector Jeff Ewans. The start was steady and it wasn't until after Hele that speed got up to the mile-a-minute mark. Then we ran well up to Whiteball, speed dropping only from 65½ after Tiverton Junction to 54½ at the top of the two miles of 1 in 155 at Whiteball summit. Even from seven coaches back I could hear the superb roar of *Nunney* up front.

We dashed down Wellington bank at or around the legal limit and tore through Taunton whistle screaming at 77mph in just 2 seconds under the booked 33 minutes from Exeter. And so it continued across the Somerset Levels, mile after wonderful mile with speed not varying very much from the maximum allowed, though challenging this for some miles as if *Nunney* just wanted to really be given her head and allowed to run. Bridgwater, scene of the flooding devastation just three short months before, was passed three minutes late and such was the tightness of the schedule that despite the fine running right up to the speed limit the lateness was still the same at Worle Junction. A fine climb of the 1 in 334/200 to Flax Bourton saw a minimum of just over 69mph and our table covered with cinders from the engine, and then a final dash for home. At Bridgwater I had doubted very much if we could possibly make Bristol on time but we ran fast down past Long Ashton at just over 77mph and it wasn't until Parson Street that the brakes came on.

And now for the usual checks I thought, but no, we ran quickly and fearlessly in past Bedminster and stopped at the London end of platform 3 half a minute early! I was delighted with this magnificent run, which is the fastest start to stop time with steam from Exeter to Bristol in the preservation era and the second fastest ever with steam, beaten only by none other than 3440 *City of Truro* on 9 May 1904, which did the stretch in 65 minutes 24 seconds!

The overall time was 70 minutes 22 seconds for the 75.49 miles, an average of 64.37mph. We had run in from Taunton in just 37 minutes 24 seconds for the 44.74 miles and had reeled off the 43 miles between mileposts 171 and 128 at an average of 76.4mph, a masterly piece

OPPOSITE: On 12 July 2008, 34067 is just past Litchfield tunnel on the Dorset Coast Express.

On 18 June 2011, 5043 storms past Hungerford with the 07.05 Solihull to Bristol.

of train running by all concerned. By comparison, the next day, 5043 during the course of its non-stop run from Plymouth had run in from Taunton in 37 minutes 11 seconds though this was to a stop at the country end of Platform 3 so the two times would probably have tied if the trains had stopped at the same place. Speeds across the Somerset levels were very similar with the *Earl* just 8 seconds faster from Taunton to Yatton, then edging slightly further ahead by dint of a faster climb to Flax Bourton (73mph minimum), to be 11 seconds ahead at Parson Street. Who could possibly have anticipated on that run in 1964 that in 2014 there

St Cross, 8 April 2014. 44932 on the empty stock of the 09.15 Ashford to Winchester.

HIGH SPEED RUNS

Engine	LMS Class 5 4-6-0 No 44932				Bulleid BB Class 4-6-2 No 34067 *Tangmere*		
Load	10 coaches, 345 tons tare, 375 tons gross				10 coaches, 334 tons tare, 365 tons gross		
Position	9 of 10				2 of 10		
GPS?	Y				Y		
	miles	mins	secs	speed	mins	secs	speed
MP 51	3.25	00	00	37	00	00	61
Wootton	4.75	01	51	46½	01	14	61½
Steventon	6.20	03	50	57	02	51	69½
Roundwood	8.45	06	06	63	04	49	67
Micheldever	10.31	07	42	69½	06	20	74
MP 59	11.25	08	33	68½	07	04	76
Weston	12.45	09	33	73	08	00	78
MP 61	13.25	10	11	75½	08	37	79
Wallers Ash	13.95	10	50	80	09	14	80½
MP 63	15.25	11	43	81½	10	07	82
Winchester Junction	16.65	12	45	78	11	06	84
MP 65	17.25	13	16	76½	11	33	84½
Winchester City	18.74	14	26	74	12	46	sigs * 61
St Cross	20.00	15	33	72½	14	01	63½
Shawford Jct	21.10	16	31	70	15	06	68
Shawford	21.88	17	06	69½	15	42	69/72
Eastleigh	25.69	20	26	64	19	47	sigs *38
	distances from Basingstoke, times from Milepost 51						

would be not one, but two steam runs of such quality on consecutive days with steam? So it was a very happy ageing train timer who caught his FGW sprinter home that evening, still speeding across the Somerset levels in his mind and reflecting on what a great day it had been.

The final two logs show the two runs I mentioned earlier where speed had been allowed to exceed the limits imposed. LMS Class 5s are limited to 60mph due to their driving wheel diameter being only 6 feet whereas Bulleids, albeit with only 2 inches more are allowed 75mph. Neither run needed much effort from the engine but both were very enjoyable and gave me speeds I thought I would never see again over one of my favourite stretches of railway.

I hope this chapter conveys the impression of what can still be enjoyed by the train timing enthusiast today, by careful selection of trip and engine to give runs as good as those enjoyed in the real days of steam. Long may it continue. The book concludes with a selection of photographs of steam working on the main line in recent years, mainly near to my home in Hampshire and a recent run on the mainline with No. 60103 *Flying Scotsman.*

On 5 September 2015, with nice white smoke, 34067 passes Totton on the Royal Wessex.

23 November 2013. Horseshoe Bridge, St Denys, 34067 *Tangmere* on the 7.25 am Weymouth to Waterloo with 47580 on the rear.

On 10 December 2012, 60163 *Tornado* passes St Cross with the empty stock of the 08.22 Peterborough to Winchester.

15 November 2008. 35028 *Clan Line* near Reculver with a VSOE Pullman.

On 7 February 2015, 46233 *Duchess of Sutherland* stands at Carlisle with the southbound CME over the Settle and Carlisle.

On 14 March 2009, 70013 *Oliver Cromwell* passes Paddock Wood with the 08.40 Waterloo to Folkestone Harbour.

LEFT: Carlisle 21 March 2015. 45690 *Leander* on the return Cumbrian Jubilee with 46115 *Scots Guardsman* on the return CME.

RIGHT: 4 October 2010 sees 60019 *Bittern* at St Cross with the 16.35 Weymouth to Waterloo.

On 27 April 2014, 34046 *Braunton* passes under Battledown Flyover with Great Britain 7.

Running as 4492, *Bittern* passes Ashurst with the Bath Spa Express from Poole to Bristol on 14 September 2011.

On the lovely crisp morning of 30 November 2011, running as 4492, *Bittern* passes Bevois Park on the Bath Spa Express from Poole to Bristol.

LEFT: 1 November 2013. Standing in for 35028, 34046 *Braunton* at Worplesdon with the Surrey Hills VSOE Pullman.

RIGHT: 46201 *Princess Elizabeth* storms out of the mist at Tilehurst with the 08.05 Paddington to Worcester.

35028 *Clan Line* passing Crofton with the Belmond Pullman to Bristol on 13 May 2015.

44871 and 45407 double head the 07.41 Ipswich to Winchester past Battledown on 9 December 2013.

On 25 February 2016. No. 60103 *Flying Scotsman* stands at Kings Cross on the 07.40 to York.

Flying Scotsman – 2016

The 25 February is quite a special day in my book, as that day in 1962 saw a valediction in the form of the final steam run around Kent, featuring a King Arthur and a Schools class on the main line sections. Fifty-four years later, on 25 February 2016, saw a new dawn for the iconic *Flying Scotsman* and its official return to the main line working after its troubled and very expensive ten-year long overhaul, which wasn't finally completed until entrusted to the capable hands of Ian Riley. I was fortunate to have been given a media pass for this event, for which I am very grateful to the NRM and Mortons Media, in particular to the editor of *Heritage Railway*. So, I found myself on the first train up from Southampton Airport in order to ensure I was at Platform One at Kings Cross by 7 am to check in and collect my pass from the very helpful staff of the NRM. That gave me plenty of time to wander up the platform to see No.67.013 bring in the empty stock of the special train, with A3 4-6-2 No. 60103 *Flying Scotsman* at the head end. The media interest was intense, of course, though I managed to secure a couple of shots and even got close enough to the cab to talk to Dave Proctor, our fireman on the first leg. His driver was Paul Major and the traction was Inspector Sean Levell, all from DBC. The stock was a mixed set of two kitchen cars, a brake with a generator for electric train heating, seven open first-class coaches and the support coach, totalling 391 tons tare for the eleven coaches, probably about 420 tons full; a good test for *Flying Scotsman*. My seat was in coach D, six back from the front and my first task was to organise the table of the four of us media bods so that I had the window seat facing the front in order to set up my gps and its aerial.

There was a general air of expectancy as we left on time and soon plunged into the darkness of Gasworks tunnel,

RETURN OF FLYING SCOTSMAN

Date	25 February 2016
Train	0740 Kings Cross to York
Loco	A3 class 7 4-6-2 No.60103 *Flying Scotsman*
Load	11 coaches, 391 tons tare, 420 tons gross
Driver	Paul Major
Fireman	Dave Proctor
Inspector	Sean Levell
Position	6 of 11
Weather	Sunny spellls, cold with light north west wind

	miles	sched	mins	secs	speed	
Kings Cross	0.00	0.00	00	00		
Copenhagen Tunnel	0.73		03	50		
Finsbury Park	2.43	8.00	08	16	8½*/12½	sigs to SL
Harringay	3.33		10	49	28	
Hornsey	3.91		12	06	32½	
Wood Green	4.88	11.30	15	18	11½*/22	
New Southgate	6.38		18	06	38½	
Barnet Tunnel	7.44		19	46	39/39½	
Oakleigh Park	8.26		21	17	32½*	slowed
New Barnet	9.09		22	28	38	
Hadley Wood	10.46		24	38	42	
Potters Bar Tunnel	10.79		25	14	42½	
Potters Bar	12.65	23.00	27	36	47½	
MP 14	13.91		29	04	55½	
Brookmans Park	14.40		29	37	55	
Welham Green	15.49		30	49	36½*/41½	
MP 17	16.91		33	00	39*	sigs
Hatfield	17.61		34	07	31*/13*	sigs
Welwyn Garden City	20.24	31.00	40	00	31½	
Digswell Jct	21.04	32.30	41	36	39/42	
Welwyn North	21.98		42	57	31*/41	slowed
Woolmer Green	23.73	36.00	45	37	39½	
Knebworth	24.91		47	17	48½	
Langley Jct	26.66		49	13	62/64½	
Stevenage	27.49	40.30	50	15	62½	
MP 29	28.91		51	33	27½*	sigs
Hitchin	31.86	46.00	55	15	32*	
Cadwell	33.21		57	13	60	
MP 34	33.91		57	48	64	
Three Counties	35.56		59	15	72½	
Arlesey	36.91		60	22	74½	
MP 38	37.91		61	11	70½	
East Road Xing	39.34		62	17	76½	
Holme Green	39.99		62	47	77½	
Biggleswade	41.10		63	38	78	
MP 43	42.91		65	05	77	
Sandy	44.04	58.00	65	59	74½/74	
MP 46	45.91		67	33	76½	
Everton Xing	46.29		67	51	75/74	
Tempsford	47.39		68	43	75	
MP 48	47.91		69	07	75½	
MP 50	49.91		70	46	72½	
			stop			
MP 51	50.84		71	56	0*	trespass
	51.00		84	46		stop
St Neots	51.61		87	53	23	
MP 53	52.91		89	49	54	
MP 55	54.91		91	50	65	
Offord Xing	55.81		92	38	69	
MP 57	56.91		93	36	67½	
MP 58	57.91		94	29	67	
Huntingdon	58.75	74.00	95	14	64	
MP 60	59.91		96	27	56½	
Stukeley	60.91		97	33	54	
Leys	61.91		98	40	53	
Abbots Ripton	63.11		100	01	60	
MP 64	63.91		100	42	66	
MP 65	64.91		101	35	69	
Woodwalton	65.91		102	59	37*	
Connington South	67.16		105	16	26*	
Connington North	67.80	86.00	106	47		water
	68.35	0.00	00	00		
Holme Xing	69.24		01	56	35½	
Yaxley	72.70		06	42	54½/57½	
Fletton Jct	74.91		09	22	32*	
Peterborough	76.25	14.00	12	40		

* brakes or speed restriction

average speed Three Counties to Milepost 50: 74.77mph

leaving the class 67 behind to follow us later. The organisers and all concerned can be highly praised for their trust in the capabilities of our steam locomotive, which wasn't misplaced. My gps, which had found a good signal while still at the platform, promptly lost it in the tunnel and it wasn't until Finsbury Park that normal service was resumed. The table sets out the running as far as Peterborough and this shows that the early stages were tortuously slow on a fine and dry, but very cold, morning. As far as I can see this was mainly due to extreme caution being shown by the engine crew (or maybe Network Rail), as the only definite reason for delay that I could identify was the check before Welwyn Garden City, where 2Y85 the 0817 to Kings Cross departed from the same platform that we used a few minutes later. By then we were nine minutes late, but with a fairly sedate schedule to the first booked stop at Holme I wasn't unduly concerned.

We got going well by Stevenage and were up to 64.3mph before we were checked again through Hitchin, but then finally were allowed to run. And run we certainly did as by Three Counties the A3 was up to 72½mph, reaching a maximum of 74½mph after Arlesey down the 1-in-400 before the hump at 1-in-264 to Milepost 38 reduced this to 70½mph. Then, down the lovely downhill stretch past Biggleswade, Sandy and Tempsford, we raced away to an average of 75.13mph over the 12 miles between Mileposts 38 and 50, starting at 70½mph and with a maximum of 78mph at Biggleswade and a minimum of 74mph after Sandy. This is clearly a very free-running engine aided by the long travel valves and 6 foot 8 inch driving wheels making it a true racehorse, which in common with No. 60163 *Tornado* ought really to be 90mph certified. Unfortunately our little romp was short lived and we made a sudden stop just short of milepost 51, for a reason which was quite obvious from the train, as spectators were scattered about along the lineside, the wrong side of the fence at this point. This was a great shame as from being nearly 10 minutes down at Stevenage, we had recovered two minutes by Sandy and I am sure would have been on time by our water stop at Holme. As it was we were at a stand for a total of nearly thirteen minutes spread over two stops, the second being quite brief. We continued in a more subdued manner but still got up to 69mph at Offord before topping the 3 miles of 1-in-200 to Leys at 53mph and running down to the water stop at Holme (actually its Connington) where we 21 minutes late. Any attempt to estimate a net time for the 67.8 miles from Kings Cross to this point would be a bit meaningless, owing to the difficulty of attributing the various early delays. Here I was served the full English breakfast (but without the champagne as train timing and alcohol don't mix) perfectly timed to coincide with the stop. We were ready to go after 16 minutes but were held at the outlet approaching Connington North for 1S09 the 0900 Kings Cross to Edinburgh to pass before regaining the main line and reaching Peterborough for a crew change over 27 minutes late.

From Peterborough crews we had Steve Hanczar in charge with fireman Jim Clarke and Traction Inspector Jim Smith. No doubt Jim Clarke's father, Don, recently retired from driving for DBS, would have been proud but maybe a little envious of his son having such a prestigious duty! We were away, nearly half an hour late, on a slow line to Stoke Junction where we were timed to wait for a succession of down trains to pass, but I had worked out that our late running should enable us to avoid this stop and so it turned out. A steady but well judged climb of the bank, with speed mainly in the mid-fifties but falling to 49mph at the top, meant we just managed to avoid the

25 February 2016. No 60103 *Flying Scotsman* after arrival at York.

pathing stop so the lateness was down to 20 minutes at Stoke Junction.

We were very close behind 1D08 the 0935 Kings Cross to Leeds, which was due to call at Grantham from 1039 to 1040, and so I wasn't surprised that, having got up to 66½mph after Great Ponton, we caught adverse signals from the Leeds train, which we were booked to precede. I also knew that, having lost our path, we were unlikely to make it as far as the next pathing stop at Carlton and so after another good spell of 75mph running down past Barkstone and Hougham, Control looped us at Claypole where a very brief stop enabled the 0948 Kings Cross to Hull to get past. This slick piece of work meant we missed out the next stop and ran through to Babworth for water. On easy gradients now, until Crow Park, *Flying Scotsman* was again worked up into speed, reaching a maximum of 76 mph before the broken climb at 1-in-200/600/200 up past The Dukeries to the summit at Markham, just before Askham tunnel pulled speed back to a minimum of 52½mph, suggesting easy working of the engine. From 16 minutes late past Newark North Gate, where the platforms were particularly crowded, we were just seven minutes late at Carlton and 12 minutes late at Babworth after a stop in the platform at Retford. Net time for the 62.72 miles from Peterborough was about 70 minutes, assuming a non stop run. Without the extra stop at Retford we would have been close to time at Babworth, but as it was the stop was prolonged as we had again lost our path. I wondered what train Control would do on a very difficult morning for them and a queue of 125mph trains all expecting to be

After arrival at York on 25 February 2016. Train crew from left; Inspector Jim Smith, Fireman Jim Clarke and Driver Steve Hanczar on No. 60103 *Flying Scotsman.*

given precedence over our 75mph steam hauled excursion, albeit a very important one. We finally got the road at midday, 25 minutes late, and restarted on a nice sunny morning behind 1N12, the 1030 Kings Cross to Newcastle, but in front of the 1035 Kings Cross to Leeds, which was right behind us and which we delayed slightly. All in all good regulating, as Control knew that we would lose the Leeds train after Doncaster. I had high hopes of an even time run to York as the 49.24 miles were only allowed 50 minutes. We made a good start along the level stretch to Scrooby, passed at 66mph and then followed the best climb of the day to Pipers Wood where the minimum on the 1-in-198 was a credible 64mph. After, speed quickly rose to 75mph down past Rossington before the engine was eased until after Doncaster where we had kept the tight 18 minute booking for the 16.73 miles from the Babworth stop. When speed had regained the seventies by Moss, I thought we were home and dry, but sadly it was not to be as lineside trespass once again intervened, this time causing another 27 minutes of delay. Great caution was shown after the restart and indeed onwards to York where we arrived into platform 9 to be met by huge crowds, just over 53 minutes late; a somewhat deflating end to a very good first official, and first solo run, with *Flying Scotsman.* After arrival I spent the next hour or so taking in the atmosphere of this special day and getting some nice shots from platform 10, opposite the one where No. 60103 had arrived and where it was sitting, the centre of an admiring crowd. All credit to those concerned with keeping this platform free of arriving

trains for the duration. Tribute must be paid to all those who have been involved in bringing this magnificent locomotive back to the main line, especially to Ian Riley and his team and, of course, to Alan Pegler, who saved her all those years ago. My sincere thanks to both train crews, to the NRM and to Virgin East Coast and Network Rail, particularly the guys in train Control, all of whom worked so hard to make this special day possible. I am sure that we are going to see some very good performances from No. 60103 in the future, hopefully without the lineside problems as the hype subsides somewhat.

No. 60103 *Flying Scotsman* storms past Horseshoe Bridge, St Denys, in the rain with the afternoon circular trip from Salisbury on 21 May 2016.